The Ultimate Guide to Residential REAL ESTATE LOANS

The Ultimate Guide to Residential REAL ESTATE LOANS

ANDREW JAMES McLEAN

JOHN WILEY & SONS
New York • Chichester • Brisbane • Toronto • Singapore

Library of Congress Cataloging-in-Publication Data

McLean, Andrew James.
The ultimate guide to residential real estate loans.

Bibliography: p.
1. Mortgage loans. I. Title.
HG2040.15.M35 1989 332.7′22 88-17319
ISBN 0471-61714-8
ISBN 0471-61713-X (pbk.)

Printed in the United States of America

10 9 8 7 6 5 4 3 2

FOREWORD

Private ownership of real property is a major part of the American dream. For most people it is the single most effective and largest investment they will ever make. In light of recent changes in the tax law, ownership of one's own home takes on new importance because, for the vast majority of us, our major tax deduction will be the interest on our mortgage loan we can write off when our tax return is filed.

Since most of us do not have the funds necessary to pay cash for the real estate we purchase, we are faced with the prospect of selecting the appropriate financing to meet our individual needs. A few years ago the choice of which mortgage loan to acquire was limited. The 30-year fixed-rate mortgage was about all that was available and purchasers of residential real estate fully understood that 360 payments or 30 years equalled home ownership.

But now the choices have become many and varied, causing confusion and consternation for the real estate buyer. We now confront such terms as ARMs, RAMs, GPMs, zero points, buy-ups, buy-downs, GEMs, wraps, AITDs. Is it any wonder that we get confused? What does all this mean and what are the positive and negative aspects of each of the loan types available in today's market?

McLean's new book, *The Ultimate Guide To Residential Real Estate Loans*, takes you on a step-by-step journey through this maze of financing, giving you a clear and concise description of the current loan types being offered throughout the country. In addition, McLean uses many examples to illustrate the effect of selecting one mortgage over another, graphically showing you both positive and negative aspects of each loan type.

In addition to a discussion of each loan type available from institutional lenders, McLean addresses the issue of seller-provided financing in its several forms. His view of this type of financing is seen from both the buyer's and the seller's perspective, and will give you some insight regardless of which side of the purchase transaction you are on.

If you are confused about what effect the new tax law may have on your personal tax position regarding real estate ownership and the resulting tax implications, you'll find the author's discussion of this topic rewarding. He has taken care to provide you with accurate up-to-date information on the new tax law. Whether you are an investor or purchasing for your own occupancy, it is information you need to know.

With all of the complexities surrounding the financing of residential real estate today, it is time someone took the mystery out of it. Andrew McLean has done just that.

Kent Harman
Assistant Vice President
Margaretten & Company, Inc.
Mortgage Bankers

PREFACE

Over the past decade so much has changed in the realm of real estate, especially finance and the income tax implications, that I found it both topical and necessary for the modern small-scale investor to have as a reference a thorough, updated handbook on real estate financing. Once I realized that the average borrower could save $30,000 or more over the lifetime of a typical mortgage loan, I knew the information I could provide in this text would be most valuable to the real estate investor.

It is intended to be a simplified, yet thorough, guide to the fundamentals of profitably financing residential real estate. I have endeavored to introduce, in plain language, ways to successfully finance a home or other real estate investment.

Both the conservative and the more daring real estate investor alike will find the information useful and enlightening.

Throughout the book examples are flavored with my own experiences, some from working in the industry and others from my own realty investments. This style of writing suits me and also serves to spice up what some might call a dry subject. Furthermore, I have attempted to inform the reader with interesting topical information as well as historical data about the subject.

The book abounds with useful knowledge and examples of how different kinds of mortgage loans work—from the standard fixed-rate loans to adjustable rate loans with convertibility and seller financing. It offers the kind of information you need to make intelligent decisions. Thus, by becoming an informed investor, you limit your risk and maximize profits on each and every real estate purchase.

This book is also unique because it features a simple, yet concise look at the latest changes in tax laws relevant to real estate. Not only have dramatic tax changes occurred, but sweeping changes in the lending business as well have also added to the complexities of investing in real estate. With this in mind, *The Ultimate Guide to Residential Real Estate Loans* attempts to provide solutions to the overflow of questions by the bewildered consumer and seasoned professional alike.

Both making money and saving money can be fun and very profitable. Although real estate has proven itself to be a safe and at times extraordinarily profitable investment, throughout the text I point out potential risks and pitfalls for the reader to avoid.

Contrary to what subscribers of the "how I made a million in two months and three days" believe, real estate investing can be hazardous to your pocketbook. It's no sure thing. Yet a well-selected, informed purchase, coupled with the best financing available, can be very lucrative and entertaining as well.

The intent of this book is to serve as a beginning study of residential real estate loans as well as a continuing guide for the experienced practitioner.

Countless persons—my students as well as friends and fellow investors—have provided valuable suggestions and contributions which, I hope, make this book informative and interesting. To these many individuals, I wish to express my sincere appreciation and thanks. Best of luck.

ANDREW JAMES MCLEAN

Las Vegas, Nevada
June 1988

CONTENTS

LIST OF ILLUSTRATIONS

TABLES

FIGURES

The Ultimate Guide to Residential REAL ESTATE LOANS

1 INTRODUCING . . . THE MORTGAGE POSSIBILITIES

Are you aware that the most expensive thing you will ever buy is not your house: It's the "cost" of the mortgage itself to acquire the house. That's right. If you borrow to buy your home, as most people do, the mortgage itself is the biggest cost item.

Because most home buyers tend to focus primarily on the monthly payment, little attention is paid to the aggregate interest costs of the mortgage. You should pay attention, because the variations in mortgage costs are, to say the least, breathtaking.

Suppose you buy a $100,000 house and borrow $80,000 at 10.5 percent for 30 years. That mortgage, if paid off over the entire 30 years, will cost you $183,448 in interest—more than double the amount you borrowed—and almost double the price of your house. And, that's not even counting the $80,000 in principal that you have to pay back. In other words, in a period of 30 years you actually paid $283,448 for a $100,000 house!

ASSUMPTION: THE BEST ALTERNATIVE

Loan assumption is, by far, the preferred method of financing real property—with two exceptions. Loan assumption is not economically feasible when the existing interest rate to be assumed is higher than the prevailing market interest rate for mortgage loans. The second exception is when the property is new construction. In the latter case, only the creation of new financing is available to the purchaser, because the builder usually has to be cashed-out from an unassumable loan position.

If your potential real estate purchase is not a new home, consider the assumption of existing low-interest rate loans which have the following advantages:

1. You can save 4 percent or more of the loan amount in loan origination fees by assuming an existing loan compared to originating a new loan. (On a $100,000 loan, that amounts to $4,000 or more in savings, not to mention the savings in lower interest rate charges.)
2. If you assume existing Veterans Administration (VA) and Federal Housing Administration (FHA) loans or certain adjustable-rate loans (and in some cases certain conventional loans), you will not have to qualify. This means no credit report or questions asked of the assumptor. (In other words, you do not need good credit.)
3. Not only are assumable loans attractive from a buyer's point of view, but when you sell, your buyer can assume the same loan —which makes your property much more saleable. (See Chapter 16, Creative Financing Strategies, for ways to use assumable loans effectively.)

PROGRAMS TO INSURE OR GUARANTEE LOANS

Another alternative, second in preference to loan assumption, is the creation of new financing backed by federal agencies.

Real estate loans are divided into two categories: loans insured or guaranteed by the federal government (in some cases, state government) and loans that are not. Loans without government support are termed "conventional" loans.

While programs under the Veteran's Administration (VA) were created to assist veteran home buyers, the Federal Housing Administration (FHA) was created to assist both homeowners and lenders alike.

VA loans are guaranteed against default and entitle qualified veterans to borrow up to 100 percent of purchase price at below market rates for homes, mobile homes, and farms.

FHA loans insure the lender against loss and entitle anyone who qualifies to borrow up to 97 percent at below market rates for certain types of real property.

During the troubled economic times of the early 1930s, both government and conventional lenders were made aware that an alternative to traditional lending practices was needed. Hence, the origin of the FHA. The FHA not only pioneered loan insurance but was also instrumental in establishing uniform loan qualification standards for prospective borrowers.

A more thorough description of VA, FHA, and conventional loans will follow later in the book.

CONVENTIONAL FINANCING

Financing that is not guaranteed or insured by federal agencies is referred to as conventional financing. This method is considered the last choice by the informed home purchaser because of the stringent requirements and costs involved. On average, a conventional loan can cost up to 4 percent or more of the loan amount for origination fees. In addition, a higher down payment is required than for government-backed loans. Furthermore, conventional lenders charge the market rate of interest, which is usually 1 percent higher than similar government-backed loans. Finally, conventional fixed-rate loans are usually not assumable, which means they are less attractive when it is time to sell.

All these mortgage possibilities as well as the different varieties of mortgage loans, such as fixed-rate and the adjustable-rate loan and the pros and cons of each, are discussed in more detail later in the book.

AFFORDABILITY

How much house you can afford depends on the type of financing you choose. New financing under VA, FHA, conventional, or adjustable-rate mortgages all have different income and down-payment requirements. Originating new financing requires much more than just good credit. Qualifying for a new loan also means you must meet certain income requirements to show the ability to pay back the loan. Essentially all these methods of financing require a range of from 25 to 33 percent of gross monthly income to be allocated for monthly mortgage payments. The higher percentage range allows for the payment of other debt obligations, including the mortgage payment.

Overall, the VA loan is the most liberal for the home buyer, as it offers the ability to purchase a home with no money down and at interest rates usually below the prevailing conventional rate. The FHA loan is the second most liberal, because it requires a small down payment—3 percent on the first $25,000 borrowed and 5 percent on the remainder. The FHA loan interest rate is also favorable when compared to conventional loan rates.

Least attractive is the conventional loan, which in most cases requires a 20 percent down payment at higher origination and interest rate cost than either the VA or FHA loans. A lesser down payment can be made under conventional terms; however, private mortgage insurance (PMI) is then required at a cost of one-quarter to one-half percent more in interest charges.

BENEFITS OF HOME OWNERSHIP

Special stock market events, such as "Black Monday" (October 19, 1987), when the market crashed 508 points in one frantic session, have served to emphasize the enduring value of owning a home (not to mention the reciprocal income tax deduction privileges of home ownership).

Most Americans prefer safe investments with historically good track records. Housing is one of those standards of enduring value, and as a result American consumers have most of their wealth invested in the homes in which they live. Investment in a home gives families a hedge against inflation; an opportunity to shelter their incomes from taxes; and, more importantly, a chance to accumulate wealth for the future.

Compare two similar families, each with two working adults and one child, a $40,000 gross income, and $10,000 to invest. One family buys a $95,000 home, investing $10,000 in the down payment and creating a $85,000 first mortgage at 10.5 percent fixed interest for 30 years. The other family continues to rent a home at $700 a month and invests $10,000 in a certificate of deposit (CD), which earns 6 percent interest compounded quarterly.

Under the assumption that family incomes, rents, and the value of the purchased home increase 5 percent a year and inflation rises 4.5 percent, at the end of the first year the homeowner pays $2723 less in federal income taxes and the value of the home will have increased by $4750, compared to a $612 gain of the renter's CD.

At the end of five years, the homeowner has paid $10,761 less in federal income taxes and the home is now worth $121,248 for a gain of $26,248. Were the homeowner to sell the home and buy another of greater value, the gain would be tax deferred. On the other hand, the renter's CD would be worth $13,457 after five years for a gain of $3457 and would be taxable.

Table 1.1 Renting Versus Owning

After One Year				
	Tax Deduction	Gain in Value	Equity Build-up	Taxes on Gain
Homeowner	$2723	$4750	$402	deferred
Renter	0	612	0	$171
After Five Years				
	Tax Deduction	Gain in Value	Equity Build-up	Taxes on Gain
Homeowner	$10,761	$26,248	$2478	deferred
Renter	0	3457	0	$968

Table 1.1 illustrates the tremendous gains attained through home ownership. Also note the equity build-up column which benefits the homeowner as the mortgage amount goes down.

From the examples given in Table 1.1 the net gain of the homeowner after five years, compared to that of the renter, is a difference of $36,998 in favor of the home ownership.

All the mortgage possibilities, including the more sophisticated adjustable-rate mortgages (some with convertability to a fixed rate), will be discussed in detail later. For now, let us try to determine how much house you can afford.

2 HOW MUCH HOUSE CAN YOU AFFORD?

The following material pertains to originating a new loan, as opposed to loan assumption. Note that although loan assumption does not require qualification (no questions asked), the borrower should still keep the loan payment within guidelines suggested for originating a new loan to avoid potential financial difficulties.

How much house you can afford depends on a lot of things. Married couples with children can afford one thing; single people usually can afford to pay proportionately more of their income toward the purchase of a home.

As a rule, couples with children should not exceed 28 percent of their gross monthly income for the house payment, including the cost of principal and interest, property taxes, and insurance. Single people and married couples with no children usually can afford up to 33 percent of gross income for a house payment.

Institutional lenders require a range of 25 to 28 percent of the borrower's gross monthly income as the limit for the house payment. This percentage, of course, can include a second income from the spousal earnings. Professional lenders know from experience what it takes to avoid financial difficulties. Therefore, it is wise to maintain your payments within these limits no matter how you acquire the loan.

Originating a new loan requires a down payment of anywhere from 5 to 20 percent of the loan amount, depending on where you get it (except for a no-money-down VA loan).

Conventional loans require a 20 percent down payment, 5 percent when PMI is used, which costs an extra half of 1 percent. FHA loans require about 5 percent down.

CLOSING COSTS

In addition to your down payment, you will be obligated to pay certain costs at closing. As a rule, total closing costs average about 4 percent of the purchase price. I have listed below items of cost that can show up on a closing statement. Some of these charges may not apply to your transaction:

- Loan origination fee. Expect to pay up to at least 2 points of the loan amount to originate a new loan.
- Loan commitment fee. Expect to pay 1 point if you want to lock in a guaranteed rate at closing. If you accept the going market rate at closing, you won't have to pay this fee.
- Escrow fee. This includes document preparation, notary services, and packaging the transaction.
- Appraisal. This is a cost the buyer customarily pays if buying under VA or FHA conditions.
- Credit report. This is a cost every borrower pays to initiate a new loan.
- Title insurance. A title policy, usually issued by a title insurance company, assures payment to any claimant in case of resolving disputes about title to the property. The cost of such is usually paid by the seller; however, sometimes the cost is split between buyer and seller.
- Recording fee
- Termite report
- Prorated taxes

In addition to the above closing costs for the buyer, the seller is obliged to pay certain closing costs.

- Sales commission
- Fees
    - Escrow
    - Recording
    - Reconveyance
    - Trust fund
    - Title insurance
- Points on government-backed loans

- Prepayment penalty
- Revenue stamps, either state or local
- Transfer taxes
- Prorated rents, taxes, and interest
- Impound account
- Documentary stamps

Closing Cost Summary

Generally speaking, creating a new loan will cost about 4 percent of the loan amount. This cost will include the incidental closing costs that pertain to your particular transaction. Bear in mind that a loan assumption can save you plenty of money. The assumption fee, by itself, is only $50. And, because you're not originating a new loan, you will save the cost of 2 percent of the loan amount just in origination fees. Finally, you will also save the cost of a credit report and appraisal, because these items are not required under a loan assumption.

Now that you have a conception of closing costs, see Tables 2.1 and 2.2, which illustrate monthly payments at selected interest rates for both 30- and 15-year fixed-rate loans. Simply select the loan amount in the left column, then go across the top and select the appropriate interest rate. Where the loan amount and interest rate intersect is the computed monthly payment for principal and interest (P&I) which you will pay to amortize the loan.

Table 2.3 shows the monthly mortgage cost of borrowing per $1000 for both 15-year and 30-year fully amortized loans at different interest rates. As an example, if you wanted to know the monthly mortgage cost of a $12,000 loan at 11 percent for 30 years, you would first look

Table 2.1 30-Year Fixed Monthly Payment (P&I) at Selected Interest Rates

Amount	Interest Rate (%)								
($)	8.0	8.5	9.0	9.5	10.0	11.0	12.0	13.0	14.0
60,000	440	461	483	505	527	571	617	664	711
70,000	514	538	563	589	614	667	720	774	829
80,000	587	615	644	673	702	762	823	885	948
90,000	660	693	724	757	790	857	926	996	1086
100,000	734	771	805	841	878	952	1029	1106	1189

Table 2.2 15-Year Fixed Monthly Payment (P&I) at Selected Interest Rates

Amount ($)	Interest Rate (%) 8.0	8.5	9.0	9.5	10.0	11.0	12.0	13.0	14.0
60,000	573	591	609	627	645	682	720	759	799
70,000	669	689	710	731	752	796	840	886	932
80,000	765	788	811	835	860	909	960	1012	1065
90,000	860	886	913	940	967	1023	1080	1139	1199
100,000	956	985	1014	1044	1075	1137	1200	1265	1332

Table 2.3 Monthly Fixed Payment (P&I) Cost Per $1000 at Selected Interest Rates

Term	Interest Rate (%) 8.0	8.5	9.0	9.5	10.0	11.0	12.0	13.0	14.0
15-Year	9.56	9.85	10.15	10.45	10.75	11.37	12.01	12.66	13.32
30-Year	7.34	7.69	8.05	8.41	8.78	9.53	10.29	11.87	11.85

for the column for 11 percent. Then select the 30-year row. The factor is 9.53. To find your monthly payment on $12,000, multiply the 9.53 factor by 12, which results in a monthly payment of $114.36.

LOAN PAYMENTS AND INCOME NEEDED TO BUY A $90,000 HOME

Since the average home in America sells for about $90,000, I felt it would be appropriate to include a table that features the payment and income required for such a house at selected rates of interest. Table 2.4 illustrates how much income you need to qualify to purchase a $90,000 house. The numbers are based on a $10,000 down payment and financing the remaining $80,000 at various fixed rates for 30 years. Annual property taxes and hazard insurance (T&I) are estimated at $120 monthly. Private mortgage insurance is not included

Table 2.4 Loan Payments and Income Needed to Buy a $90,000 Home

Rate (%)	Monthly P&I	Monthly T&I	Total PITI	Annual Income to Qualify
8	$587	$120	$707	$30,000
9	644	120	764	32,743
10	702	120	822	35,229
11	762	120	882	37,800
12	823	120	943	40,414
13	885	120	1005	43,071
14	948	120	1068	45,771

for the purpose of simplicity. The total monthly payment, which includes principal, interest, taxes, and insurance (PITI), is based on 28 percent of the minimum qualifying monthly income.

Mortgage Cost Worksheet

To determine the amount of monthly mortgage cost you will have to pay, follow this procedure:

Step 1

Fill in the following blanks:

Home purchase price $ ____________

Less the down payment ____________

Mortgage loan amount ____________

Term of loan ____________

Step 2

To determine the mortgage loan amount in thousands, divide the mortgage loan amount by 1000 and enter result on line (a).

Mortgage loan amount ________ divided by 1000 = ________ (a)

From Table 2.3, look up the appropriate cost factor per $1000 for your mortgage's rate of interest and term. (For example, the cost per $1000 at 11 percent for 30 years is $9.53.)

Enter your cost per $1000 on line (b). ____________ (b)

To calculate your monthly principal and interest payment, multiply line (a) by line (b) and enter the result on line (c).

Monthly P&I cost ____________ (c)

QUALIFYING FOR A NEW LOAN

When you finally think you're ready to ask for a loan . . . stop—take a deep breath—and prepare yourself for quite an ordeal, especially if the loan you're applying for is government-backed. Conventional loans usually can be processed in 30 days; VA and FHA loans can take anywhere from 60 to 120 days. (Bureaucratic red tape and additional inspections usually add to the time required on government-backed loans.)

Whatever the case, you can help speed up the loan approval process by carefully obtaining and submitting information required by the lender.

When you initiate the loan request, the lender will start the process by having you fill out the loan application. If you have all the pertinent information required on the loan application, go ahead and fill it out completely. If not, take the application home, fill it out, and either mail it or personally return it to the lender.

In addition to the loan application, you will be required to sign an employment verification form. The lender will submit this signed form to your employer to verify your employment. It is advisable for you to alert the person responsible to the coming inquiry.

If you are self-employed, it will be necessary to supply the lender with federal income tax returns for the past two years and a profit and loss statement since your last tax filing.

From the information on the loan application, the lender will order a credit report. Once the credit report is made available to the lender, it will be carefully scrutinized. If your credit is not approved, you will be informed of the bad news.

When the lender receives the appraisal and title report, he will analyze both, then determine the maximum amount he will lend on the property. Next the lender takes into account your income to see if the monthly payment falls within stipulated guidelines. (Remember, a maximum of 28 percent of your gross income is allowed for principal and interest, taxes, and insurance.) If it does, you will then be informed of this amount and the amount of points and interest rate the lender will charge.

In certain cases, additional steps are taken in the loan process. Under VA and FHA requirements, a property inspection is required in order to determine if the property meets certain minimum standards. Also, certain states require a termite inspection of the property.

The following loan application (Figure 2.1) shows what information the lender will require of you. If you are self-employed, the lender will require you to fill out a profit and loss and balance sheet. (See Figures 2.2 and 2.3.)

RESIDENTIAL LOAN APPLICATION

MORTGAGE APPLIED FOR	☐ Conventional ☐ FHA ☐ VA ☐	Amount $	Interest Rate %	No. of Months	Monthly Payment Principal & Interest $	Escrow/Impounds (to be collected monthly) ☐ Taxes ☐ Hazard Ins. ☐ Mtg. Ins. ☐

Prepayment Option

SUBJECT PROPERTY

Property Street Address	City	County	State	Zip	No. Units

Legal Description (Attach description if necessary) | Year Built

Purpose of Loan: ☐ Purchase ☐ Construction-Permanent ☐ Construction ☐ Refinance ☐ Other (Explain)

Complete this line if Construction-Permanent or Construction Loan	Lot Value Data / Year Acquired	Original Cost $	Present Value (a) $	Cost of Imps. (b) $	Total (a + b) $	ENTER TOTAL AS PURCHASE PRICE IN DETAILS OF PURCHASE.

Complete this line if a Refinance Loan

Year Acquired	Original Cost $	Amt. Existing Liens $	Purpose of Refinance	Describe Improvements [ ] made [ ] to be made Cost: $

Title Will Be Held In What Name(s) | Manner In Which Title Will Be Held

Source of Down Payment and Settlement Charges

This application is designed to be completed by the borrower(s) with the lender's assistance. The Co-Borrower Section and all other Co-Borrower questions must be completed and the appropriate box(es) checked if ☐ another person will be jointly obligated with the Borrower on the loan, or ☐ the Borrower is relying on income from alimony, child support or separate maintenance or on the income or assets of another person as a basis for repayment of the loan, or ☐ the Borrower is married and resides, or the property is located, in a community property state.

BORROWER	CO-BORROWER
Name / Age / School Yrs	Name / Age / School Yrs
Present Address No. Years ☐ Own ☐ Rent	Present Address No. Years ☐ Own ☐ Rent
Street	Street
City/State/Zip	City/State/Zip
Former address if less than 2 years at present address	Former address if less than 2 years at present address
Street	Street
City/State/Zip	City/State/Zip
Years at former address ☐ Own ☐ Rent	Years at former address ☐ Own ☐ Rent
Marital Status ☐ Married ☐ Separated ☐ Unmarried (incl. single, divorced, widowed) — DEPENDENTS OTHER THAN LISTED BY CO-BORROWER: NO. / AGES	Marital Status ☐ Married ☐ Separated ☐ Unmarried (incl. single, divorced, widowed) — DEPENDENTS OTHER THAN LISTED BY BORROWER: NO. / AGES
Name and Address of Employer — Years employed in this line of work or profession? ___ years; Years on this job ___; ☐ Self Employed*	Name and Address of Employer — Years employed in this line of work or profession? ___ years; Years on this job ___; ☐ Self Employed*
Position/Title / Type of Business	Position/Title / Type of Business
Social Security Number*** / Home Phone / Business Phone	Social Security Number*** / Home Phone / Business Phone

GROSS MONTHLY INCOME

Item	Borrower	Co-Borrower	Total
Base Empl. Income	$	$	$
Overtime			
Bonuses			
Commissions			
Dividends/Interest			
Net Rental Income			
Other† (Before completing, see notice under Describe Other Income below.)			
Total	$	$	$

MONTHLY HOUSING EXPENSE**

	PRESENT	PROPOSED
Rent	$	
First Mortgage (P&I)		$
Other Financing (P&I)		
Hazard Insurance		
Real Estate Taxes		
Mortgage Insurance		
Homeowner Assn. Dues		
Other:		
Total Monthly Pmt.	$	$
Utilities		
Total	$	$

DETAILS OF PURCHASE

Do Not Complete If Refinance

a. Purchase Price	$
b. Total Closing Costs (Est.)	
c. Prepaid Escrows (Est.)	
d. Total (a + b + c)	$
e. Amount This Mortgage	( )
f. Other Financing	( )
g. Other Equity	( )
h. Amount of Cash Deposit	( )
i. Closing Costs Paid by Seller	( )
j. Cash Reqd. For Closing (Est.)	$

DESCRIBE OTHER INCOME

B–Borrower C–Co-Borrower	NOTICE: † Alimony, child support, or separate maintenance income need not be revealed if the Borrower or Co-Borrower does not choose to have it considered as a basis for repaying this loan.	Monthly Amount
		$

IF EMPLOYED IN CURRENT POSITION FOR LESS THAN TWO YEARS COMPLETE THE FOLLOWING

B/C	Previous Employer/School	City/State	Type of Business	Position/Title	Dates From/To	Monthly Income
						$

THESE QUESTIONS APPLY TO BOTH BORROWER AND CO BORROWER

If a "yes" answer is given to a question in this column, explain on an attached sheet.	Borrower Yes or No	Co-Borrower Yes or No	If applicable, explain Other Financing or Other Equity (provide addendum if more space is needed).
Have you any outstanding judgments? In the last 7 years, have you been declared bankrupt?			
Have you had property foreclosed upon or given title or deed in lieu thereof?			
Are you a co-maker or endorser on a note?			
Are you a party in a law suit?			
Are you obligated to pay alimony, child support, or separate maintenance?			
Is any part of the down payment borrowed?			

*FHLMC/FNMA require business credit report, signed Federal Income Tax returns for last two years, and, if available, audited Profit and Loss Statements plus balance sheet for same period.

**All Present Monthly Housing Expenses of Borrower and Co-Borrower should be listed on a combined basis.

***Neither FHLMC nor FNMA requires this information.

FHLMC 65 Rev. 8/78 FNMA 1003 Rev. 8/78

REVERSE SIDE OF THIS FORM ON OPPOSITE PAGE →

Figure 2.1. Loan application

This Statement and any applicable supporting schedules may be completed jointly by both married and unmarried co-borrowers if their assets and liabilities are sufficiently joined so that the Statement can be meaningfully and fairly presented on a combined basis; otherwise separate Statements and Schedules are required (FHLMC 65A/FNMA 1003A). If the co-borrower section was completed about a spouse, this statement and supporting schedules must be completed about that spouse also. ☐ Completed Jointly ☐ Not Completed Jointly

STATEMENT OF ASSETS AND LIABILITIES

ASSETS		LIABILITIES AND PLEDGED ASSETS			
		Indicate by (*) those liabilities or pledged assets which will be satisfied upon sale of real estate owned or upon refinancing of subject property			
Description	Cash or Market Value	Creditors' Name, Address and Account Number	Acct. Name If Not Borrower's	Mo. Pmt. and Mos. left to pay	Unpaid Balance
Cash Deposit Toward Purchase Held By	$	Installment Debts (include "revolving" charge accts)		$ Pmt./Mos.	$
				/	
Checking and Savings Accounts (Show Names of Institutions/Acct. Nos.)				/	
				/	
Stocks and Bonds (No./Description)				/	
				/	
Life Insurance Net Cash Value *Face Amount ($)*				/	
SUBTOTAL LIQUID ASSETS	$	Other Debts Including Stock Pledges		/	
Real Estate Owned *(Enter Market Value from Schedule of Real Estate Owned)*		Real Estate Loans		X	
Vested Interest in Retirement Fund					
Net Worth of Business Owned (ATTACH FINANCIAL STATEMENT)					
Automobiles (Make and Year)		Automobile Loans		/	
Furniture and Personal Property		Alimony, Child Support and Separate Maintenance Payments Owed To		/	X
Other Assets (Itemize)				/	X
		TOTAL MONTHLY PAYMENTS		$	X
TOTAL ASSETS	A $	NET WORTH (A minus B) $		TOTAL LIABILITIES	B $

SCHEDULE OF REAL ESTATE OWNED (If Additional Properties Owned Attach Separate Schedule)

Address of Property (Indicate S if Sold, PS if Pending Sale or R if Rental being held for income)	⇩	Type of Property	Present Market Value	Amount of Mortgages & Liens	Gross Rental Income	Mortgage Payments	Taxes, Ins. Maintenance and Misc.	Net Rental Income
			$	$	$	$	$	$
		TOTALS →	$	$	$	$	$	$

LIST PREVIOUS CREDIT REFERENCES

⇩ B-Borrower C-Co-Borrower	Creditor's Name and Address	Account Number	Purpose	Highest Balance	Date Paid
				$	

List any additional names under which credit has previously been received ____________

AGREEMENT: The undersigned applies for the loan indicated in this application to be secured by a first mortgage or deed of trust on the property described herein, and represents that the property will not be used for any illegal or restricted purpose, and that all statements made in this application are true and are made for the purpose of obtaining the loan. Verification may be obtained from any source named in this application. The original or a copy of this application will be retained by the lender, even if the loan is not granted. The undersigned ☐ intend or ☐ do not intend to occupy the property as their primary residence.

I/we fully understand that it is a federal crime punishable by fine or imprisonment, or both, to knowingly make any false statements concerning any of the above facts as applicable under the provisions of Title 18, United States Code, Section 1014.

____________ Date ________ ____________ Date ________
Borrower's Signature Co-Borrower's Signature

INFORMATION FOR GOVERNMENT MONITORING PURPOSES

Instructions: Lenders must insert in this space, or on an attached addendum, a provision for furnishing the monitoring information required or requested under present Federal and/or present state law or regulation. For most lenders, the inserts provided in FHLMC Form 65-B/FNMA Form 1003-B can be used.

FOR LENDER'S USE ONLY

(FNMA REQUIREMENT ONLY) This application was taken by ☐ face to face interview ☐ by mail ☐ by telephone

____________ ____________
(Interviewer) Name of Employer of Interviewer

FHLMC 65 Rev. 8/78 REVERSE FNMA 1003 Rev. 8/78

REVERSE SIDE OF THIS FORM ← ON OPPOSITE PAGE

Figure 2.1. Continued

SIMPLIFIED
PROFIT AND LOSS STATEMENT

January 1, 19___
to
December 31, 19___

RECEIPTS		$40,000.00
COST OF SALES		
Beginning Inventory	$ 3,500.00	
Purchases	22,000.00	
	$25,500.00	
Less: Ending Inventory	2,000.00	
TOTAL COST OF SALES		23,500.00
GROSS PROFIT		$16,500.00
EXPENSES		
Payroll	$10,000.00	
Advertising and promotion	1,000.00	
Accounting	500.00	
Insurance	800.00	
Taxes	500.00	
Repairs and maintenance	800.00	
Supplies	1,000.00	
TOTAL EXPENSES		$14,600.00
OPERATING PROFIT		1,900.00
LESS DEPRECIATION		500.00
NET PROFIT		$ 1,400.00

Figure 2.2. Simplified profit and loss statement

SIMPLIFIED BALANCE SHEET

ASSETS		**LIABILITIES AND NET WORTH**	
CURRENT ASSETS		CURRENT LIABILITIES	
Cash on hand and in banks	$	Notes payable	$ ....
Accounts and notes receivable (Less Reserve for Bad Debts)	....	Accounts payable	....
Inventories	....	Taxes:	
TOTAL CURRENT ASSETS	$______	Federal income tax	....
		Real estate personal property	....
FIXED ASSETS		Payroll taxes payable	....
Land, buildings, and machinery and equipment (Depreciation value)	$	Sales tax payable	....
TOTAL FIXED ASSETS	$______	Miscellaneous	....
		TOTAL LIABILITIES	$______
OTHER ASSETS		*TOTAL NET WORTH	$______
Goodwill	$		
TOTAL ASSETS	$______	TOTAL LIABILITIES AND NET WORTH	$______

*Total NET WORTH. This figure is determined by subtracting the *total accrued liabilities* from the *total assets*. Adding total net worth to the "Liabilities and Net Worth" column will cause both sides to be in balance.

Figure 2.3. Simplified balance sheet

3 INTEREST RATES AND MONEY

Frequently, especially in the recent history of the economy, funds available for real estate loans have suddenly become scarce. In just a matter of months, mortgage money seemingly disappears and the overall money supply also appears to dry up. This scarcity of money inhibits the strength of the economy; it slows down construction, makes it more difficult for potential homeowners to finance mortgages, and, consequently, reduces the income of those working in the real estate industry.

What causes this scarcity in the money supply? The answer is directly related to changes in the interest rate and the stimulating policies of the Federal Reserve System.

THAT'S "INTEREST"–ING

Before the Federal Reserve is discussed, a definition is in order. *Interest* is the rate a lender charges a borrower for the service of lending money. Or, in other words, it is the amount of return (yield) on investment expressed as a percentage.

Interest rates have more of an impact on the overall economy and inflation than anything else. Just a 1 percent increase in the lending rate can disqualify half-a-million potential home buyers from the loans they need to buy a home. The stock market is especially vulnerable to changes in the rate of interest charged by lenders.

How inflation, interest rates, and the money supply are controlled is described in the following section on the Federal Reserve System.

THE FEDERAL RESERVE SYSTEM

Enacted in 1913 by Congress, the Federal Reserve Act established 12 federal reserve districts, with a federal reserve bank in each district. The Federal Reserve System, commonly referred to as the "Fed," has the primary purpose of influencing the cost, the availability, and the overall supply of money, and consequently the rate of interest.

When the Fed initiates policies which make money scarce (a "tight" money policy), interest rates rise. A policy by the Fed to add funds to the money supply acts to reduce the rate of interest.

Both inflation and deflation are thought to be directly related to the rate of interest. Thus, the Fed will raise or lower the rate of interest in an attempt to control the forces of either inflation or deflation which are affecting the economy at a particular time.

Briefly, *inflation* is defined as the cost of goods and services increasing faster than the income of the consumer purchasing these things. *Deflation* is essentially the opposite, the price of goods and services decreasing in relation to the money available to buy them.

It is the thinking of the Fed that in order to decrease the rate of inflation, it will increase the rate of interest. To offer an example, suppose someone wishes to construct a building and rent the available space. The return is estimated to be 10 percent per year; therefore, the building will pay for itself in 10 years. The cost of borrowing the money to build is 7 percent. If this is the case, the person would proceed with the project because a 3 percent profit will be made.

This builder's actions, combined with those of other business people developing similar projects, will instigate inflationary pressures on the price of certain necessary, but relatively scarce, supplies to build these projects.

Therefore, the Fed believes that if they raise the interest rate to 8 percent, this entrepreneur, along with other developers, will reconsider and decide not to go ahead with a project. The additional costs of higher interest payments would reduce profits too much. The net result is an absence of inflationary pressure on the supplies required to build these projects.

If the Fed were concerned about deflation, it would act in an opposite manner—they would lower interest rates to make the development of these projects more profitable.

How Interest Rates Are Shifted

In order to raise interest rates to control the forces of inflation, there are five procedures available to the Federal Reserve System: (1) adopt a restrictive open market policy; (2) increase the discount rate; (3) increase reserve requirements; (4) when approved by Congress, adopt selective controls; and (5) apply moral suasion.

Restrictive Open Market Policy. Through the Fed's open market committee, it has the right to buy and sell government bonds to banks. Should the Fed make the bond interest rate more attractive, banks will purchase these bonds, resulting in fewer dollars available in banks for loan purposes. In this case, money will become scarce. Now bankers will become more selective in their lending procedures, and, because they have the opportunity of buying more government bonds with no risk and little handling cost, they will begin increasing the rate of interest on the lendable money they have left.

For example, suppose the Fed issues a 9 percent bond. On average, it costs a bank 0.5 percent to handle a mortgage loan; thus, in order for a bank at least to break even, it must charge a minimum 9.5 percent interest on a mortgage loan. Unless the banker can earn more than 9.5 percent, he will refrain from originating mortgage loans and will purchase more government bonds. Therefore, by making money scarce, the interest rate is increased. The end result will be that inflationary pressures will be reduced as proposed building projects are abandoned because of the higher cost of borrowing money.

Increase the Discount Rate. When a bank borrows from a federal reserve bank, the rate of interest it must pay is referred to as the "discount rate." In fact, what the member banks actually do is take certain promissory notes and discount them with the Federal Reserve; with the cash received, the member banks underwrite more loans. If the discount rate is increased, it often means that it no longer pays to discount these notes. Consequently, money is no longer borrowed from the Fed, which eventually leads to a scarcity in the supply of money available for lending purposes. Inevitably, interest rates will increase because of the scarcity of lendable money.

Increase Reserve Requirements. Regulations require the U.S. banking system to hold in reserve a certain fraction of its deposits. This means that banks, by law, are not allowed to lend out 100 percent of their deposits—only a portion of them.

For example, suppose the reserve requirement is 20 percent. If a bank receives a $1000 deposit, it is required to deposit at least 20 percent in the federal reserve bank in its district. This deposit is referred to as the "legal minimum-reserve balance," and it consists of a stipulated amount of both demand deposits (checking accounts) and time deposits (savings accounts). The Fed is authorized to set certain minimum and maximum reserve requirements. Should it decide to raise the reserve requirement from 20 to 25 percent, a bank can lend out only $750 from a $1000 deposit instead of $800 under the 20 percent reserve requirement.

As you can see, the Fed can raise interest rates by raising reserve requirements which results in making scarce the money available for loans.

Selective Controls. On occasion, Congress is authorized to provide specific terms to constrict or expand credit terms. One specific example of this occurred in 1950 under the Defense Production Act which authorized Congress to limit certain aspects of real estate financing. Under this act the Fed increased down-payment requirements on homes and reduced the time of maturity on mortgage loans.

Although this act was repealed in 1953, it is representative of restrictive selective control. By putting certain limits on real estate financing, the Fed reduced the number of eligible home buyers from the market. Similar to the other steps used by the Fed, this act helped to reduce inflationary pressure.

Moral Suasion. Finally, during inflationary periods the Fed will sometimes try to persuade member banks to tighten credit policies. This is an attempt by the Fed to discourage unsound credit policies (speculation) that are inconsistent with conservative (prudent) banking philosophy.

A PARTIAL HISTORY OF INFLATION

Once upon a time there was a place where a three-bedroom house cost $17,200. The interest rate on the loan was 5.5 percent—and all you needed was a job and a down payment of $860 to move in. You could put a new Chevy Impala in your two-car garage for $2700, and, for the small change of less than a dollar, you could purchase a six-pack of beer. Believe it or not, a first-run movie was $1.50, a candybar was a nickel, and, more important, a dollar was worth a dollar.

This place that sounds like a very inexpensive place to live was, of course, the United States, and the once-upon-a-time was not so long ago—1967. It was also a very turbulent time in U.S. history, although by today's standards it was a time when the price of Chevrolets and home ownership seemed reasonable.

Since 1967, the United States has experienced some of the worst inflation in its history, especially in the late 1970s and early 1980s. In 1970 the Bureau of Labor Statistics began measuring inflation, using 1967 as its base.

Using sophisticated computers, weighted logarithms, and super-subindexes, the Bureau has confirmed what most of us have felt in our checkbooks: Items that cost $10 in 1967 now cost $34, on average.

Wages have also increased since 1967, and with two breadwinners (both husband and wife working), these families are enjoying purchasing power far exceeding the single wage earner families of a generation ago. Today, many Americans are willing to pay for cars what they paid for houses in 1967.

Table 3.1 Selected Mortgage Interest Rates—1950 to 1988

Date	*Percent*
April, 1950	4.25
April, 1953	4.50
December, 1956	5.0
August, 1957	5.25
September, 1959	5.75
May, 1961	5.25
October, 1966	6.00
August, 1973	8.25
April, 1979	10.00
April, 1980	14.00
May, 1980	11.50
March, 1981	14.00
September, 1981	17.00
October, 1982	12.50
May, 1984	14.00
January, 1987	8.50
April, 1987	9.50
September, 1987	10.50
February, 1988	9.50
July, 1988	10.50

Table 3.1 shows the recent history of selected home mortgage interest rates from 1950 to 1988. Notice how much they have increased, especially from April 1979 to September 1981. This was a period in U.S. economic journals when the effects of inflation were most extreme. (The higher interest rates during this period was an attempt by the Fed to counteract these inflationary pressures.) These fluctuating interest rates have dramatic effects on the real estate market, as well as the stock market.

INTEREST RATES CAN CHANGE QUICKLY

What makes interest rates fluctuate? First, consider that the function of the lending institution in giving you the loan is that of making an investment. It is investing a sum of money to achieve a fixed or variable rate of return for a set period of time.

Since these companies are in the business of making new loans and none has an unlimited supply of money, they systematically sell these loans, or package of loans, in the open or "secondary" market. How much these loans are sold for depends upon how much other investments are selling for and what investors think the investments may do in the near future.

Let's say that today you apply for a real estate loan. The lender quotes you a fixed-rate loan at 10 percent for 30 years. It is likely that within 30 days the same lender would quote an entirely different rate. The reason for the fluctuation in rate of interest quoted is due to a delicate balance among investments being offered in the secondary mortgage market. If one of these investments becomes more attractive than your mortgage's yield, then the cost of your loan will go up. Conversely, if other investments become less attractive, then the cost of your mortgage will go down.

When your loan rate becomes less attractive, mortgage market investors require some "premium" to attain a higher yield. The premium is added to the loan amount in the form of discount points. When these points are added to the loan, the loan package becomes attractive again.

The components that shape the future for interest rate-related investments are constantly changing. Factors such as inflation, our national debt, trade imbalance, and the price of oil and gold all have their effect on interest rates.

Interest Rate Trends

Interest rates follow a trend over an extended period, then usually change direction and maintain a new directional trend. This constant ebb and flow creates profitable opportunities for those who can predict the direction interest rates are heading.

As recently as the autumn of 1987 interest rates were headed in an upward direction. Events in the stock market eventually had a major effect in altering this upward direction of interest rates.

INTEREST RATES AND BLACK MONDAY

Monday, October 19, 1987, has been dubbed "Black Monday" by historians because of the record-breaking losses suffered by stock market investors. It was a historic Monday as the Dow Jones Industrial Average plummeted 508 points on record volume, all in one single day. This dramatic loss in value wasn't measured in millions nor in billions of dollars—it was measured in "trillions of dollars." (In case you don't know, a trillion dollars is a thousand billion dollars.)

This spectacular sell-off was one of historic proportions: 22.6 percent in total value lost in the stock market in a single trading session. This tremendous break in prices was five times greater than any previous daily loss in the same market, including the infamous Black Friday that precluded the Great Depression of 1929.

Now I will describe the scenario leading up to the stock market crash of Monday, October 19, 1987. The stock market had been on a historic bull-run lasting over five years. Interest rates were also on the rise, which normally, by itself, can send the market tumbling. Yet, the market seemingly ignored these soaring interest rates and continued to climb.

Besides rising interest rates, investors began fretting about two other things in particular: the trade imbalance (recently reported at a record high) and the federal budget deficit. Both items have been twin towers of worry for investors over the years, especially the federal budget deficit, because nothing was being done to correct it.

Now, if you combine all this terrible economic news (rising interest rates coupled with a record trade imbalance and federal budget deficit) mixed in with an over-bought stock market, a price correction of major proportions had to occur.

The seemingly frenzied selling opportunity presented itself after investors had a chance to ponder all that bad news over the weekend leading up to Black Monday. Remember, though, this stock market had just recorded all kinds of record highs and had endured five years of a very profitable bull-run. Therefore, when the market began to crumble, it had a long distance to fall because it had previously run up to such a record high.

Before this classic day in stock market annals, interest rates were in a rising trend with conventional fixed-rate loans going for 11.5 percent, up substantially from previous offerings.

Concerned about implications of the stock market crash, the federal government initiated policies that it felt would stimulate economic activity and curb the fear of a possible recession. Besides the politicians who promised to correct the federal deficit, the Federal Reserve began stimulating procedures that within a few days reduced conventional mortgage interest rates from 11.5 to 10.5 percent. (VA and FHA rates also fell to 9.5 percent.)

In conclusion, it would be difficult to determine exactly "who" is responsible for the losses of Black Monday. "Who" is likely to be a combination of a number of participants and/or factors. However, if anybody is to receive blame, it has to be the federal government (both past and present) and its policies regarding the federal budget deficit. What's it doing to be blamed? Spending what it doesn't have!

If a private business used the same business practices of continually spending what it doesn't have, it would eventually go bankrupt. If the federal government continues to spend without cutting back, it eventually has to go bankrupt in theory. Yet the government can print more money to pay for its debt (which it has been doing for two generations), and now the world economy is saying, "If you don't control spending what you haven't got, you'll have to pay the price."

MONEY RATES

The selected money rates shown in Table 3.2 are quotations reflecting market conditions on any given day. Most of these rates are published daily in the business section of many leading newspapers.

Types of Rates

□ *Prime Lending Rate.* This is the most favorable interest rate charged by commercial banks to its best customers. The prime rate is often used as a base on which to set an entire class of loans. For example, mortgage loans are likely to be quoted to a borrower at one point over the prime rate or construction loans at two points over prime. Most

Table 3.2 Money Rates

Prime lending	8.50%
Fed discount	6.00%
Mortgage Rates	
30-year fixed (FHLMC)	9.94%
30-year adjustable (FHLMC)	7.64%
15-year fixed	9.90%
Treasury Security Rates	
3-month T-Bill discount	5.63%
6-month T-Bill discount	5.85%

banks usually set their own prime lending rate; however, most will follow one of the leading commercial banks.

□ *Treasury Bill Rate.* Treasury Bills (T-Bills) are sold by the Fed at weekly auctions and can be purchased from the bank or through authorized security dealers. T-Bills are sold at minimum increments of $10,000; interest rates on these bills are quoted on a weekly basis.

The yield on T-Bills is expressed as a discount because it is the difference between the purchase price and the face value of the bill. For example, a $10,000 six-month T-Bill could be purchased recently for $9527, returning a yield of 9.95 percent. At maturity, the return of $10,000 would earn $473 for six months' use of the money.

The T-Bill rate is an excellent guide to the trend in the short-term rate of money market funds. As an example, consider the following news item on March 7, 1988 from *USA Today*. "T-Bill Yields Fall: The Treasury sold $6.4 billion in three-month bills at an average discount rate of 5.63 percent, down from 5.74 percent last week. Another $6.4 billion was sold in six-month bills at an average discount rate of 5.85 percent, down from 6.11 percent last week."

□ *Federal Funds Rate.* This is the rate of interest charged by one bank to another for money loaned on a short-term basis. When a bank's cash reserves fall below federal regulations because of prior loan commitments, it can call on another bank that may have a cash surplus and is willing to make a short-term loan.

The interest rate charged varies from state to state, but the importance of this rate in relation to mortgage money is that the Fed watches it carefully in regulating the entire money supply. Should the federal funds rate increase over that of the previous week without the Fed's adding money into the system to help reduce the rate, it is a true indication that the policy of the Fed is to tighten the money supply, which eventually would cause all interest rates to rise over the short term.

□ *FNMA Auction Yield.* This is the rate at which the Federal National Mortgage Association (FNMA) will buy home loans over a four-month period. The FNMA holds auctions every second Monday, expressing an actual yield at which it will purchase home loans if the originator of the mortgages cannot get a better price elsewhere. The yield quoted is a consensus rate of what the participating lenders on that particular day would pay for mortgages over the next four months.

Lender expectations over the next four months for home loan rates tend to be reflected by the yields quoted. The following Tuesday after each auction, acceptance bids are published representing the purchase of large blocks of loans that will accurately indicate the future of home mortgage interest rates.

□ *Annual Percentage Rate (APR).* APR is the actual cost of credit to the consumer in precentage terms. Regulations in the Truth in Lending Act require that borrowers are to be informed of the cost of credit to allow comparison of costs based on a uniform rate—the Annual Percentage Rate.

The finance charge and the APR are really the two most important disclosures required under Truth in Lending. These two items tell the customer, at a glance, how much is being paid for credit and its relative cost in percentage terms.

At one time, a lender may have offered a consumer loan of $1000 at 6 percent interest for a term of one year. The borrower was then charged $60 for the loan, it was deducted from the $1000, and the remaining balance of $940 was given to the borrower. Since the actual effective interest rate on $940 paying back $1000, is in effect 6.38 percent, not 6 percent. This is one of the major reasons truth in lending came into existence.

TRUTH IN LENDING

The Truth in Lending Act came into law several years ago with the purpose of disclosing to consumers the actual cost of credit. Two important disclosures regarding real estate loans are the APR and the fi-

KISS YOUR LANDLORD GOODBYE

Buy Your Dream House For Less

Than You're Paying In Rent!

7.5%

ACT NOW!

A.R.M. Adjustable Rate Mortgage. Maximum increase of 2% per year, 5% over term. 8.125 APR. Subject to change over term of loan. Also available are 9% conventional 30-year fixed-rate loans with 10% down.

Figure 3.1. Sample advertisement

nance charge. Now the consumer/borrower can avoid the uninformed use of credit by comparing relative costs at a glance. From the sample advertisement in Figure 3.1, note the full disclosure of the copy describing the available financing; yet, the advertiser informs the customer of the actual cost of credit which is 8.125 percent APR.

Figure 3.2 is a sample form issued to the borrower. Truth in Lending requires the lender to inform the borrower of the APR and all related costs involved with the loan.

YIELD

Yield is defined as return on investment, or the ratio of income from an investment to the total cost of the investment over a given period.

The true meaning of yield in relation to all types of real estate loans

REAL ESTATE LOAN DISCLOSURE STATEMENT

BROKER/ARRANGER OF CREDIT: ______________________ CREDITOR: ______________________

(Name) ______________________ (Name) ______________________

(Address) ______________________ (Address) ______________________

Purpose of Loan: ______________________

I. Loan in the amount of $__________ is to be secured by a note and Deed of Trust in favor of Creditor on property located at ______________________, which is ☐ is not ☐ expected to be the location of the Borrower's principal residence. (NOTE: If it is, a Rescission Statement must be provided unless this transaction involves a first lien for the purchase or initial construction of a dwelling.)

The Deed of Trust may secure additional advances and may cover after-acquired property. The loan may also be secured by an assignment of proceeds from any required insurance protecting the property.

II. Charges included which are not part of the Finance Charge:

1. Appraisal .... $______
2. Credit report .... $______
3. Notary .... $______
4. Recording .... $______
5. Title insurance .... $______
6. Document preparation .... $______
7. Property insurance .... $______
8. Termite inspection .... $______
9. Other__________ (Describe) .... $______

Total Charges.......... $______

Property insurance may be obtained by Borrower through any person of his choice. If it is to be purchased through the Broker or Creditor, the cost appears at Item II. 7 above.

Credit life and disability insurance are not required to obtain this loan.

III. FINANCE CHARGE:

A. Prepaid **FINANCE CHARGE**

Broker's commission .... $______

Loan escrow fee .... $______

Other__________ $______

__________ (Describe) $______

(Total of A) $______

B. Interest for period of loan.................... $______

FINANCE CHARGE (A + B $______

Finance Charge accrues from ______________________, 19______

IV. AMOUNT FINANCED:

Amount of loan from Item I (Includes all charges in Item II which are not paid in cash)..... $______

Less Prepaid **Finance Charge** (Item III. A).................... $______

AMOUNT FINANCED $______

V. **ANNUAL PERCENTAGE RATE:** __________%

VI. PAYMENT TERMS:

Payable in __________ payments of principal and interest as follows: __________

monthly instalments of $__________ each, beginning __________, 19______, and a final/balloon payment of $__________ due on __________, 19______

TOTAL OF PAYMENTS (Item I + Item III. B) $______

There are no arrangements for refinancing balloon payments.

If any payment is not made within __________ days after it is due, a late charge must be paid by Borrower, as follows: ______________________

On prepayment in full, unaccrued interest is cancelled and a prepayment charge will be computed, as follows: ______________________

I HAVE READ AND RECEIVED A COMPLETED COPY OF THIS STATEMENT.

Date: ______________________, 19______ ______________________ (Borrower)

______________________ (Spouse)

Figure 3.2. Real estate loan disclosure statement

is often not properly understood by lenders, borrowers, and real estate investors.

Let's make one point very clear: Determining the yield on many loans is far more complex than a mere division problem. The calculation itself can be so complex that it requires the use of a computer or computer-prepared factors. Because the formula is too complex to fully explain, I will attempt to offer a simple example of computing yield.

A person borrows $1000 for one year and at the end of that year $100 interest is paid. That is based on a 10 percent interest rate and it's also a yield of 10 percent. A key point here is that yield is always expressed as an annual figure.

Why is the yield and the interest rate the same? Because there were no payments made whatsoever, the term of the loan was a full year, and at the end of that year a certain amount is paid for the use of that money.

To determine the yield, divide the cost of money by the amount borrowed, as follows:

$100 ÷ $1000 = 0.10 or 10 percent interest rate or yield

The only time the yield is determined by simple division is when no payments are made, the term is a full year (or two or three full years, etc.), and there are no extra charges such as loan origination fees, escrow fees, etc.

Now we can explore a similar loan problem that is more complex.

Consider that $1000 is borrowed for one year and $8.33 interest is paid each month for 11 months with a final payment of $8.33 plus the $1000 borrowed. However, an extra fee of $50 is required by the lender to process the loan. As a result, the borrower receives only $950 of the loan proceeds. Since borrowing a specific amount and receiving less complicates the problem, let's review this.

The interest paid is still $100 (12 × $8.33) for one year's use of the money. The interest of $100 should not be divided by $950 to get a yield of 10.53 percent because it can only be used on terms of one year. The interest rate is 10 percent (100 divided by 1000); however, the yield must show the relationship of the interest paid ($100), the amount borrowed ($1000), the extra fees paid ($50), and when the interest and fees are paid. This requires a complex formula as mentioned earlier.

Since you must spread the $50 loan fee over a one-year period, the yield in this case is 15.43 percent. (This calculation and the following yields are taken from Mortgage Yield Tables.) If the same payment is made for two years instead of one and the loan fee and amount of loan remain the same, the yield is then 12.85 percent. The effect of the loan fee is spread out over a two-year versus a one-year term. For a three-year term, the yield would be less than 12 percent, 11.99 percent to be exact.

One is not expected to understand the mathematics involved (few do), only the concept that extra fees (over and above interest) increase the cost of the loan and increase the yield or true annual percentage rate.

The whole area of borrowing a specific amount of money, yet receiving less, will always affect the yield. In the above problem, $1000 was borrowed and only $950 was received. This leads into a whole area of yields on discounted notes and mortgages.

SELLING DISCOUNTED NOTES

An individual can sell a note to an investor by a method similar to that used by a bank to sell a package of loans (notes) to an investor. Let's say you possess a note owed to you by someone else. The note is for $10,000 at 10 percent interest-only (payment of interest and no payment on principal until terms end), payable monthly for five years. You received this note a year ago when your house was sold and you took back a second mortgage using the home as security for the loan. Now, you can sell this note to an investor converting your monthly interest payments to a lump sum of cash.

That's right. Notes owed to you are worth cash and are definitely considered a negotiable instrument. How much your note is worth depends on a number of factors. Those primary factors relevant to determining the value of a note are: interest rate, quality of the security, and term of the loan.

Prospective investors who buy second mortgages require a certain yield. It is common to see a note discounted 25 percent or more in order to provide the desired yield. In other words, the $10,000 note mentioned earlier would be discounted $2500 (25 percent of $10,000). Thus, the investor would buy the note for $7500. During the life of the note it would pay 10 percent interest-only until maturity, at which time the $10,000 originally owed on the note would be due.

Generally speaking, the greater the discount, the higher the yield.

LEVERAGE

Leverage is the ability to use a small amount of cash to acquire a sigificantly greater value in assets. *Zero leverage* would be a full cash purchase, as opposed to a 10 percent down payment with 90 percent financing, which would be a purchase 90 percent leveraged. The more leverage used means more yield on your invested dollars.

For example, let's assume you have the option of paying $50,000 cash for a house or you could put 10 percent down ($5000) and leverage (finance) the remaining balance. Let's now compare the resuits to see the amount of yield from the two transactions.

A year after the purchase you determine that the value of the house increased $5000 (10 percent) to $55,000. If you put only $5000 down on the property, the resulting yield would be 100 percent ($500 gain divided by investment). If a full cash price is paid, $50,000 is invested; when that figure is divided into the gain of $5000, the yield is a meager 10 percent. (Also, the tax ramifications have to be considered since interest payments are tax deductible.)

As you can see, the value of leverage is very important to profitable real estate investment.

Paying cash for properties also has its merits, especially when the investor can purchase properties substantially below market value. Then the buyer can refinance a cash purchase in order to recoup the majority of the cash investment. (For more information on this type of financing, see Six-Month-Rollover, 100 Percent Financed in Chapter 16, Creative Financing Strategies.)

To succeed and profit at real estate investing, one must view the financing of real estate as a joint venture with lenders; however, as the investor, you don't have to share with the lender the profits realized—you are only required to pay back the loan with interest.

Giant corporations with a surplus of cash often finance their real estate purchases so as to improve their return on investment through leverage.

4 FINANCIAL TERMINOLOGY

Before we dig deeper into the realm of real estate finance, you should familiarize yourself with the more common financial instruments and terms used in the industry today. (See additional words in Glossary.)

MORTGAGES AND DEEDS OF TRUST

Mortgages and Deeds of Trust are financial instruments that create liens against real property. These instruments state that, should the borrower default on the loan (fail to make payments when due), the lender has the legal right to sell the property in order to satisfy the loan obligation in a foreclosure sale.

There are two parties involved in a mortgage: the *Mortgagor*, or the borrower and property owner, and the *Mortgagee*, or the lender. There are also two parts to a mortgage: the *Mortgage Note*, which is evidence of the debt, and the *Mortgage Contract*, which is security for the debt. The note promises to repay the loan; the contract promises to convey title of the property to the mortgagee in case of default.

Trust Deeds (Deeds of Trust) are similar to mortgages except that an additional third party is involved and the foreclosure procedures are simpler. Under a trust deed the borrower, or owner, is called the *Trustor*. The lender is referred to as the *Beneficiary*. The intermediate third party, whose responsibility is to hold title to the property for the security of the lender, is referred to as the *Trustee*.

Under a trust deed, if the trustor defaults on the loan obligation, the subject property will be sold at public auction by the trustee through provisions in the "power of sale" clause contained in the trust deed, *without court procedure*.

Foreclosure is initiated by a notice of default, which is recorded by the trustee with a copy sent to the trustor. If after three months the trustor does nothing to remedy the situation, a notice of sale is posted on the property and advertisements of the sale are carried in local newspapers once a week for three weeks. If during this period the trustor fails to pay the beneficiary sufficient funds to halt the foreclosure, the sale will be conducted by the trustee. Proceeds from the foreclosure sale are first disbursed to the beneficiary, then to any other lien holders according to their priority.

Foreclosure under a mortgage instrument, as opposed to a trust deed, is notably longer (periods in excess of a year are common). For this reason more than half the states in the United States prefer the trust deed over a mortgage instrument.

Second trust deeds and mortgages (or thirds, fourths, and so on) are similar to firsts, except that they are second in priority to a first loan with respect to security and their ability to claim any proceeds from a foreclosure sale.

DIFFERENCES BETWEEN ASSUMED, SUBJECT-TO, AND TRANSFERRED MORTGAGES

There are important differences in the meaning of these terms. An *Assumed Mortgage* occurs when the borrower assumes the legal obligation to make the loan payments and the lender releases the previous borrower from the liability. Assumption then, technically speaking, can legally take place only *in the absence of a due-on-sale clause.*

Buying the property *Subject-To* the existing mortgage occurs when the buyer takes over the loan obligation but the existing borrower is not released from the liability and formal arrangement with the lender is not made. Caution should be taken when buying property subject to the existing mortgage—especially when a due-on-sale clause is involved—because the legality of enforcement of the due-on-sale clause differs in each state.

An *Assigned Mortgage* is one that you already own. It is an asset or a negotiable instrument that has value. It is also a note that someone is paying you principal and interest on, and your security is the mortgage against certain property. As your down payment, you could assign (transfer) this mortgage to the seller of the property you wish to acquire.

Finally, be aware of *Due-on-Sale* and *Alienation* clauses written into loan documents. Without going into great detail, they essentially mean the same thing: If the title to the property transfers to another person, the lender can call the total remaining amount due and payable within 30 days. Or the lender has the right to ask for assumption fees and an increased rate of interest. Most conventional loans contain these clauses and therefore are not assumable. On the other hand, FHA and VA loans do not have these clauses, which makes them very attractive, especially if the interest rate is below the market interest rate; they are fully assumable in most cases, without any credit qualification whatsoever.

See Figures 4.1, 4.2, and 4.3 for samples of important documents. Pay special attention to Figure 4.1. A full reconveyance is issued only when the original note, the deed of trust securing it, and a request (Figure 4.3) signed by all owners of the note, together with the reconveyance fee, are surrendered to the trustee for cancellation.

PREVENTING FORECLOSURE

Communication with the mortgage lender is the key to avoiding the act of foreclosure. If you happen to fall behind in mortgage payments, don't procrastinate. There are several alternatives, and the sooner you do something about it the more options you have in solving your financial dilemma.

NOTE SECURED BY DEED OF TRUST

(INSTALLMENT—INTEREST INCLUDED)

$______ __________, California, __________

In installments as herein stated, for value received, I promise to pay to __________

__________, or order,

at __________

the sum of __________ DOLLARS,

with interest from __________ on unpaid principal at the rate of ______ per cent per annum; principal and interest payable in installments of __________ Dollars

or more on the ______ day of each ______ month, beginning on the ______ day of __________

__________ and continuing until said principal and interest have been paid.

Each payment shall be credited first on interest then due and the remainder on principal; and interest shall thereupon cease upon the principal so credited. Should interest not be so paid it shall thereafter bear like interest as the principal, but such unpaid interest so compounded shall not exceed an amount equal to simple interest on the unpaid principal at the maximum rate permitted by law. Should default be made in payment of any installment of principal or interest when due the whole sum of principal and interest shall become immediately due at the option of the holder of this note. Principal and interest payable in lawful money of the United States. If action be instituted on this note I promise to pay such sum as the Court may fix as attorney's fees. This note is secured by a DEED OF TRUST to TITLE INSURANCE AND TRUST COMPANY, a California corporation, as Trustee.

__________ __________

__________ __________

THIS FORM FURNISHED BY TITLE INSURANCE AND TRUST COMPANY

Figure 4.1. Note secured by deed of trust

Pg. 1 of 2

NOTE SECURED BY DEED OF TRUST

INSTALLMENT NOTE – INTEREST ONLY

$______________________________, California,______________________________, 19____

In installments as herein stated, for value received, I promise to pay to ______________________________

______________________________, or order,

at ______________________________

the sum of ______________________________ DOLLARS,

with interest from ______________________________ on unpaid principal at the rate of

______________ per cent per annum, payable in installments of ______________________________

______________________________ Dollars

or more on the ______________ day of each ______________ month, beginning on the

______________ day of ______________, 19____. ______________________________

____

and continuing until ______________________________ at which time the entire principal balance together with interest due thereon shall become due and payable.

Should default be made in payment of any installment of principal or interest when due the whole sum of principal and interest shall become immediately due at the option of the holder of this note. Principal and interest payable in lawful money of the United States. If action be instituted on this note I promise to pay such sum as the Court may fix as attorney's fees.

______________________________ ______________________________

______________________________ ______________________________

Note secured by deed of trust (page 2)

______________________________, California

______________________________, 19____

For value received, I hereby transfer and assign to

____

the within Note and the Deed of Trust securing the same, so far as the same pertains to said Note, without recourse. ______________________________

Interest to accrue from

____

By ______________________________

PAYMENTS

DATE PAID M	D	Y	DATE DUE M	D	Y	Amount Paid	Interest Paid To	CREDITED ON Interest	CREDITED ON Principal	Balance Prin. Unpaid	To Whom Paid

Figure 4.2. Note secured by deed of trust (interest only)

Request for Full Reconveyance

Date:..

The undersigned owns and holds.....................promissory note............for the sum of $..................................

....dollars, and all other indebtedness secured

by a Deed of Trust dated..19.........., made by..

....

Trustor, recorded..19.........., File No.................................. in Book..............................

Page..........................., Official Records of...County, California.

You are notified that all indebtedness secured by said Deed of Trust has been fully paid; and you are directed upon surrender to you for cancellation of said Deed of Trust and note or notes, and upon payment to you of any sums owing to you under the terms of said Deed of Trust, to reconvey without warranty to "the person or persons legally entitled thereto" the estate now held by you and acquired through said Deed of Trust.

This space for use by Trustee.
REGISTER NO..............................
Clerk..............................
Reconveyance issued..............................
Checked by..............................
Delivered..............to..............................
Note and Trust Deed Cancelled..............................

Address for mailing of reconveyance:..............................

Figure 4.3. Request for full reconveyance

Contrary to what some people think, most mortgage lenders prefer not to foreclose. Taking possession of defaulted real estate is only a means of last resort. A mortgage lender's intention from the beginning is simply to earn a profit by lending money on secured real estate, not to become a defaulted owner and overseer of foreclosed real estate.

Mortgage lenders, especially in certain economically depressed areas of the country, will do just about anything, within reason, to avoid foreclosure. Suppose, for example, a borrower becomes ill and is unable to work for three months. The borrower should call the lender and explain the situation. The lender might agree to accept a reduced loan payment or, possibly extend the loan term.

Why mortgage lenders, especially in economically depressed areas, try to avoid foreclosure is evidenced by recent events in the petroleum-producing industry.

During the mid-1980s, cities such as Houston and Dallas, Texas suffered severely from drastically reduced oil prices. An over-supply of oil in the world market caused huge reductions in both prices and production, which eventually caused severe cutbacks in employment. The repercussions were felt all over the state as more unemployed oil workers began defaulting on their mortgage payments.

Lenders began to foreclose. But, because the entire area was so economically depressed, there were not enough available buyers (at almost any price) to buy the foreclosed real estate. The final result was a record number of bank failures, which essentially was caused by a glut in the supply of petroleum in the world market (not to mention the glut of unsold homes in Houston and Dallas).

A similar scenario occurred in Detroit, Michigan when U.S. car makers experienced bad economic times because of intense foreign competition. (In this particular situation, banks did not experience the tremendous losses that Texas suffered, but the severity of a so-called rolling recession hurt the job market just the same.)

In the mid-1970s gasoline prices were rising through the roof. Detroit was building big, heavy, gas-guzzling cars, while the Japanase, who already were producing top-quality, gas-efficient, smaller cars at home, began selling them in the United States. The U.S. consumer was impressed with the practical Japanase cars and began buying them in great numbers. It was several years before the U.S. car manufacturers could shift over to producing smaller, more gas-efficient cars that matched the quality of the Japanese cars. The tremendous loss in sales for U.S. car manufacturing caused a severe economic depression in Detroit that was felt for several years after.

Although Detroit banks did not suffer as much financially as did the Texas banks during the oil-price crisis, the housing market along with employment definitely suffered. This goes to illustrate an old cliché, "When General Motors sneezes, Detroit catches a cold."

Other Alternatives to Foreclosure

Another alternative available to those with FHA loans is loan assignment. In certain cases, the Department of Housing and Urban Department (HUD), of which the FHA is part, can be assigned the loan. In such cases, HUD will work with the troubled borrower in an attempt to arrive at an affordable payment plan.

Finally, if financially troubled borrowers can't find another solution, they can attempt to give the deed back to the mortgage holder in order to avoid foreclosure. In Nevada, this is called "a deed in lieu." It simply means the borrower is giving up all interest in the house to save the lender the hassle and cost of going through the normal procedure of foreclosure in order to receive a deed.

Borrowers should be aware that if foreclosure occurs and the property is sold for less than what is owed on the mortgage, the lender can seek a "deficiency judgment" against the borrower, and that both it and a deed in lieu will mar the borrower's credit.

5 TYPES OF REAL ESTATE LOANS

Real estate loans can be classified in several different ways. One means of classification is according to the plan of repayment of the loan that the borrower and lender agree upon. The basic repayment plans available are:

Interest-only (straight-term) loans
Amortized loans
Partially amortized loans
Adjustable rate loans
Graduated loans

INTEREST-ONLY LOANS

Also referred to as the "straight-term" or "balloon" loan, this particular loan requires the payment of interest-only during the term of the loan. At the end of the term, the entire principal is due and payable in one final balloon payment. For example, the annual payment schedule for a interest-only loan for $40,000 at 10 percent interest for a term of five years is as follows:

Example of an Interest-Only Loan

1st year	$40,000 × .10	= $ 4000 interest
2nd year	$40,000 × .10	= $ 4000 interest
3rd year	$40,000 × .10	= $ 4000 interest
4th year	$40,000 × .10	= $ 4000 interest
5th year	$40,000 × .10	= $ 4000 interest
Total interest paid		= $20,000
Balloon payment		= $40,000
Total principal and interest		= $60,000

Prior to the Great Depression of 1929, the interest-only loan was the most common payment method for real estate financing. Many borrowers took out these loans for short terms and expected to renew them term after term, thus deferring payment of the principal almost indefinitely. But when the entire world economy failed, most lenders were unable to "roll-over" or perpetuate these interest-only loans. The results were devastating. Lenders began calling loans, requiring the borrowers to pay the entire principal amount owing, which they did not have. Lenders began foreclosing on these loans throughout the country.

The Great Depression made almost everyone, especially those in the financial industry, aware of the inherent dangers in this type of financing. A more practical form of loan soon materialized in the amortized loan.

FULLY AMORTIZED LOANS

An alternative to the interest-only loan is the fully amortized loan, featuring equal payments over its term, applied to both principal and interest. In contrast to the interest-only loan, the fully amortized loan commonly has a term of 30 years or more and is completely paid off at the end of its term.

Initial payments on the amortized loan consist mostly of interest. As the loan matures, more of each payment is applied toward the principal, since interest on an amortized loan is calculated on the loan's outstanding principal balance. After each payment, the principal balance is reduced, resulting in a smaller interest portion and a larger principal portion of the overall payment.

Table 5.1 is an example of a $5000 fixed-rate loan at 10 percent interest fully amortized over five years. The monthly payment required to amortize such a loan is $106.24 (taken from payment tables) including principal and interest. Note that the original loan balance is $5000 plus one month's interest, or $5041.67.

The monthly interest is calculated as follows: the principal amount owing times 10 percent divided by 12 months. The principal amount owing is then reduced each month by the amount of each payment applied against it. The amount of interest charged each month gets smaller, which means the amount of principal applied to the loan balance increases with each payment. The equity build-up is the amount of principal paid off each month.

Table 5.1 Example of How a $5000 Loan Is Amortized at 10 Percent for 5 Years

Loan Balance	Interest (Monthly)	Loan Balance & Interest	Payment	Principal (Monthly)	Payment No.
5000.00	41.67	5041.67	106.24	64.57	1
4935.03	41.13	4976.56	106.24	65.11	2
4870.32	40.59	4910.91	106.24	65.65	3
4804.67	40.04	4844.71	106.24	66.20	4
4738.47	39.49	4777.96	106.24	66.75	5
4671.72	38.93	4710.65	106.24	67.31	6
4604.41	(loan balance after 6 payments)			395.59*	

Note how monthly interest is added to the loan balance, then the regular monthly payment is deducted, resulting in a new loan balance.
*Accumulated equity (principal) build-up after six payments.

How to Calculate Interest Paid on Amortized Loans

Lending money is a very competitive business and not all mortgage lenders charge the same rate of interest. When making a loan many variables come into play: the lender's profit margins, the cost of the lender's own money supply, the loan amount, and duration of the loan. Because of the large amount of money borrowed on real estate mortgages and their lengthy durations, just a slight difference in the rate of interest can mean a difference of thousands of dollars over the life of the loan.

On a standard amortized loan, the total interest paid is calculated as follows: The mortgage payment (taken from payment tables) is multiplied by the total number of payments. The result is the total amount of principal and interest paid. Subtract the face value of the loan from the total to find the interest paid.

Example: Let's say you have a $70,000 loan at 10 percent fixed rate to be repaid in monthly payments of $614.31 over a term of 30 years. How much interest will have been paid at maturity (when the loan is fully amortized, or paid off)?

Solution:

1. $614.31 monthly payment × 12 months = $7371.72 annual payment

2.	$7371.72 annual payment	×	30 years	=	$221,151.60 total payment

3. Total principal and interest paid $221,151.60
   Less loan amount −70,000.00
   Equals total interest paid $151,151.60

Now, let's say the same loan can be obtained at 9 percent, instead of 10 percent. Here's how to figure the total interest paid over 30 years:

Solution at 9 Percent:

1.	$563.24 monthly payment	×	12 months	=	$6758.88 annual payment
2.	$6758.88 annual payment	×	30 years	=	$202,766.40 total payment

3. Total principal and interest paid $202,766.40
   Less loan amount −70,000.00
   Equals total interest paid $132,766.40

A 9 percent as opposed to a 10 percent rate results in a savings of $18,385.20 in interest paid over 30 years.

PARTIALLY AMORTIZED LOANS

The partially amortized loan is similar to the fully amortized loan, except that a balloon payment is due at the end of the term. This type of loan allows the borrower a smaller payment on the loan and to pay off some of the principal owing. It is popular when the seller finances his equity in the property under a purchase-money second mortgage.

As an example, a partially amortized loan could have the following terms: $80,000 loan at 10 percent amortized over 30 years at $702.06 per month, but payable in 20 years. Thus, at the end of 20 years the borrower would owe a balloon payment of approximately $53,000. If the loan were payable in 30 years it would be fully amortized with a zero balance. ($53,000 is an approximate balance taken from loan progress tables.) Normally, such a loan for 20 years would require a monthly payment of $772.02 to fully amortize it. Since the borrower's payment is $702.06, there is a savings of $69.96 per month; however, a substantial balloon will be left at end of the term.

ADJUSTABLE-RATE LOANS

Adjustable-rate mortgages (ARMs) originated a few years ago to protect long-term lenders from radical changes in market interest rates. Traditionally, conventional lenders had lent their funds at reasonable interest rates, and rightly so as their cost of acquiring that money seldom fluctuated. But along came the hyperinflationary times of the mid-1970s and the 1980s, and the cost of money to lend out went up dramatically. At the same time these lenders had loaned billions of dollars at interest rates substantially below what it cost them to acquire these funds. Thus, the adjustable-rate mortgage.

ARMs vary somewhat, but basically they are similar. The rate of interest on the loan is allowed to fluctuate over the entire term of the loan. For example, if the interest rate originates at 9 percent, it is allowed to increase up to 5 points to a limit of 14 percent, with a maximum increase of 2 percent during any 12-month period. Typically, the amount of interest rate charged is tied to some government index, such as the federal discount rate; if the federal discount rate goes up, the ARM interest rate goes up, but not to exceed 2 points in one year and not to exceed 5 points over the term of the loan.

Usually a borrower can originate an ARM at a lower interest rate than for a fixed-rate loan, mainly because of the reduced risk to the lender. However, the borrower must realize that the interest rate of the ARM may increase 5 points over the term of the loan. For instance, on a loan of $80,000 at 9 percent for 30 years, the principal and interest payment would be $643.71. For the same loan and term at 14 percent (the 5 percent maximum increase allowed), the principal and interest payment would be $947.90, or a monthly increase of $304.20. Over the entire term of 30 years, that's a difference of $109,512. As you can see, ARMs represent a substantial and significant risk to the borrower. (See Chapter 9 for more details.)

GRADUATED LOANS

Also known as the Graduated Payment Mortgage (GPM), this plan offers smaller initial loan payments which become larger as the term goes on. This type of loan anticipates the borrower's expectation of income growth to meet the GPM's schedule of increasing payments.

The FHA Graduated Loan is being terminated at the end of 1988. Because of the excessive risk inherent in graduated loans, the reader should avoid these types of loans.

LOAN UNDERWRITING

The process of risk evaluation is termed "underwriting." Lending on real estate involves considerable amounts of money, and frequently the money a lender loans is borrowed money—money that is likely to be in a savings account entrusted to the lender's safekeeping. Therefore, it is very important that the lender carefully evaluate the risk before lending a considerable amount of money to just "anybody" to finance a specific property.

A loan underwriter must evaluate three basic items: the borrower, the property, and the location.

The borrower is required to fill out a standard loan application, which includes questions about income and financial condition. From the loan application, the lender evaluates the borrower's ability to repay the loan. In addition, the lender will order a credit report and an appraisal of the subject property.

The borrower must demonstrate not only ability to repay the loan, but also a desire to repay. From the credit report the borrower's credit history is brought to the attention of the lender. Past-due bills, judgments, collection agency notices, foreclosure, and bankruptcy are all evidence of a borrower's poor credit.

Next, the lender evaluates the security (collateral) for the loan, the property itself. The written appraisal is examined to determine the property's market value and a title report is ordered to uncover liens or other information against it.

Finally, the property's location is evaluated. The lender considers the presence of adequate utilities, street paving, and distance from shopping and recreational faculties. Proximity to schools and public transportation are also considered. Outside forces (economic obsolescence) that can cause a decline in the subject property's value are also evaluated, such as the intrusion of industrial developments into the area, declining values in the surrounding neighborhoods, or changes in zoning.

All these items have a bearing on the lender's final decision to approve or disapprove a loan, as does the amount of down payment invested by the borrower. The smaller the down payment, the more money the lender has to lend, which means more risk for the lender and less risk for the borrower. Also, if the borrower defaults and the lender is forced to foreclose, there is a greater risk that the lender cannot recover the full interest in the property because of a smaller down payment.

Loan-to-Value Ratio

The customary term to describe a ratio or relationship between the amount of down payment and the value of the property is the *loan-to-value ratio* (LTVR). The LTVR allows the lender to determine the limits of how much may be lent on a particular property within set guidelines.

To calculate the LTVR, divide the loan amount by the property's appraised value or selling price, whichever is less. The resulting LTVR is expressed as a percentage, as in the example that follows.

Example of LTVR. The loan amount is $60,000 and the appraised value is $75,000, however the property is sold for $77,000. Therefore, to determine LTVR the loan amount is divide by appraised value, not the selling price.

$$\$60{,}000 \div \$75{,}000 = .80 = 80\% \text{ LTVR}$$

As a rule, lenders generally require a minimum 80 percent LTVR on owner-occupied property. For nonowner-occupied property, lenders usually require a 70 percent LTVR. In other words, institutional lenders usually require the owner to have a minimum 20 percent equity interest in the property before underwriting a loan on owner-occupied property and at least a 30 percent equity interest in non-owner-occupied property.

I recently received a solicitation from a home loan company advertising home equity loans (see Figure 5.1). From the sample advertisement, note that the LTVR is more conservative (70 instead of 80 percent, which most lenders will give on owner-occupied property). Also note that if you know what the lender's LTVR is, you can determine the amount you are eligible to borrow. Simply multiply the LTVR by the value of your home, then deduct the balance owed on your first mortgage and the result is the amount you can borrow. If you also owe on a second mortgage, the lender is likely to use a portion of the loan proceeds to pay it off. This way the new lender can maintain a secondary position and avoid being in third position behind an existing secondary note holder.

I have used this type of financing when I purchased several properties and the seller carried back a second mortgage. In one particular case I owed $17,000 on a second mortgage payable interest-only at 10 percent with a seven-year maturity. The first mortgage was $15,000 at 7 percent. Three years after I purchased this house, the holders of the second mortgage told me they would accept $14,000 (worth $17,000

CONVERT YOUR EQUITY

INTO CASH

USE YOUR EQUITY AS SECURITY FOR A LOAN

EXAMPLE:

Estimated Selling Price	$85,000
Percentage We Loan	70%
	$59,500
Less Balance Owed on First Mortgage	39,500
You Can Borrow This Amount	$20,000

IN THIS EXAMPLE THE EQUITY IN YOUR HOME IS $20,000

We offer fully amortized loans at fixed rates with no repayment penalty and fully assumable.

Loan-to-value ratios: 70% owner-occupied, 65% nonowner-occupied, and 50% land (all types).

Figure 5.1. Sample advertisement

at maturity in four years) for the note if I paid it off within six months. Anxious to save $3,000, I applied for, and received, the necessary home equity loan.

The following is an example of that transaction:

Estimated value	$50,000
Percentage they'd loan (LTVR)	70%
	$35,000
Less balance owed on first mortgage	15,000
This is the amount I borrowed	$20,000

Of this amount borrowed, $14,000 was used to pay off the existing second mortgage holder; the remaining $6000 was for my personal use. By the way, I was charged 11.5 percent interest plus 2 points in origination fees, which is substantially higher than the 10 percent rate I was paying. However, the note I owed was discounted $3000 which more than offset the higher costs of the new loan.

Discount Points

Both the Veteran's Administration (VA) and the Federal Housing Administration (FHA) set the maximum permissible interest rate that can be charged the buyer on their particular loans, with one exception: the FHA has no ceiling on the maximum rate. Frequently, this maximum rate is pegged below interest rates charged by conventional lenders in the open market. To provide an incentive to originate VA and FHA loans, lenders are permitted to equalize the difference between pegged rate and open market rates by charging discount points.

To calculate discount points, the lender will first deduct the VA or FHA rate from the open-market interest rate. As an example, assume the following interest rates are in effect:

Open market interest rate	11.0%
FHA fixed interest rate	10.5%
Difference	0.5%

Based on past studies on the average life of a mortgage, it has been established that each 1 percent difference in interest rates equals 8 discount points. (A 1 percent difference equals 8/8 discount points.) Thus, a 0.5 percent difference in interest rates equals 4/8. To originate the loan from the preceding example, the lender would charge 4 points, or 4 percent of the loan amount.

Buyers under VA loan programs are usually not permitted to pay these discount points and therefore they are paid by the seller in most cases. However, the lender is not prohibited from charging another form of points, called "service points," on all types of loans.

Similar to a discount point, a service point represents 1 percent of the loan amount. (Maximum allowed by VA and FHA is 1 percent.) These service points often referred to as "loan origination fees," are incorporated into the loan to increase the lender's yield without raising the interest rate. As with interest rates, what lenders charge in service points tends to fluctuate according to supply and demand of money available to lend.

LOAN COMMITMENTS

For loan brokers, builders, and others who depend on mortgage funds to operate efficiently, it is necessary that lenders make certain types of promises or loan commitments for available funds. The procedures and terminology may vary throughout the country but the intention of each form of commitment tends to be rather uniform. The following categories describe such loan commitments.

Future Commitment

This form of commitment is used in pledging funds for a building yet to be constructed. It may include terminology such as "on or before September 30, 1988," or it may encompass a time span, such as "this loan commitment cannot be exercised before 12 months nor later than 24 months from date of this agreement." The future commitment is a pledge of a certain specified amount of money to be made available at a later specific date.

Actual use of the money funded under a future commitment is not mandatory; however, if the holder of the commitment finds a cheaper source of funding elsewhere, the commitment fee is forfeited.

The lender usually charges a fee—a total of 1 to 2 points of the funds promised—for pledging funds at fixed-interest rates at some future date and perhaps rightly so, as interest rates have fluctuated so much in the past.

Forward Loan Commitment

This form of commitment is usually between a lender and mortgage company which also spells out the type of loan and conditions the lender will accept. In addition, it describes the services provided by the mortgage company and the fees charged for such services.

Under this type of promise, a specific amount of money is available for certain types of loans at a fixed rate of interest. The mortgage company is authorized to collect a service charge of one-tenth to one half of 1 percent of the loan for providing loan escrow services, handling collections, and paying taxes and insurance. Usually the term of this commitment set by the lender does not extend beyond six months.

The commitment fee, if required, is usually 1 percent of the funds committed and is due at the time of issuance of the commitment. Normally the commitment fee is refundable when the pledge is 100 percent utilized. Should the entire commitment not be fully used, the mortgage company may be required to forfeit a portion of the fee.

Take-Out Commitment

This form of money pledge, also referred to as a "stand-by commitment," is used for any kind of proposed construction. It is a commitment that is actually a back-up promise because it is never intended to be used but is available if needed. It is used most often during tight money conditions and is issued at an interest rate higher than the prevailing market rate. Usually the developer will have three to five years to exercise an option to use the commitment at a cost of 2 to 4 points of the promised funds.

The true purpose of a take-out commitment is to assure the developer of construction financing, just in case funding is not available through a construction loan. The developer would forfeit the commitment fee if a more reasonable permanent loan were obtained.

Permanent Loan Commitment

This is the final mortgage loan which is amortized over a term of up to 40 years. On a single-family residence, a permanent loan is made to the buyer as an immediate commitment or a future commitment is made prior to construction of the house.

Before a commercial development can begin, a permanent loan or a valid take-out commitment must be assured before a construction loan can be funded.

6 LOAN ASSUMPTION

Loan assumption has the primary advantage of saving money; however, there are many other notable advantages. Before these positives are brought forth, let's take a brief look at loan assumption.

LOAN ASSUMPTION AT A GLANCE

- One small assumption fee, about $50, is the only cost as compared to 4 points or more to originate a new loan.
- You assume an interest rate lower than that of the prevailing market rate, thereby getting a lower monthly payment.
- No qualification is required. In other words, you do not need good credit (no questions asked).
- The loan you assume is subsequently assumable by another buyer, which makes your property more salable.

WHAT LOANS CAN BE ASSUMED?

Existing VA and FHA loans and certain conventional loans without a due-on-sale clause are fully assumable without qualification by the buyer. However, certain FHA loans issued on or after December 1, 1986, have special exceptions. For assumed FHA loans that were issued on or after the above date, a mandatory credit check is required if the loan is assumed within the first 12 months for owner occupants and within 24 months for investors. In addition, if the original mortgagor does not get a release from the mortgage, the buyer and seller will have joint liability for five years after the assumption. These provisions do not include FHA loans issued before the above-mentioned date.

PROS AND CONS

Assumption of existing low-interest-rate loans saves time and money —lots of money. On the typical long-term loan of 20 years or more, loan assumption could save you $30,000 or more on the average purchase.

Not only does loan assumption save you money on lower interest-rate payments but the cost to assume is much less than the cost of loan origination. Loan assumption is usually just $50, whereas the total cost of loan origination can be 4 points or more of the loan amount. On an $80,000 loan that's at least $3200. The following are certain loan closing costs you avoid when a loan is assumed: title search, credit report, appraisal, and points. The 2 to 3 points of the loan amount charged for loan origination is the major cost.

On a typical $80,000 loan assumption, then, you can save $3150 compared to loan origination ($3200 less $50 assumption fee). That's a tremendous savings, not to mention the time and convenience of assumption. More savings occur later in the life of the loan because an assumed loan, in most cases, has a lower rate of interest than a new loan.

Not only is loan assumption attractive from a buyer's point of view but as a seller you have a built-in advantage because the loan you assumed as the buyer will be fully assumable when you sell.

Finally, one often-overlooked advantage of loan assumption over other methods of financing is that an assumption takes only a few days to close as opposed to 60 to 90 days or more to conclude other methods of financing. Although conventional lenders are, at times, efficient and both the VA and FHA are beneficial to a prosperous real estate market, red tape associated with these agencies leads to borrower frustration. When I say 60 to 90 days to close a real estate deal, I'm being conservative. I've had a VA deal take forever, and I've had an FHA deal take up to six months to close.

Why does it take such a long time to process a loan? Primarily, it is because processing a loan is a giant paper shuffle, especially for VA and FHA loans. A conventional loan doesn't take as long because there are fewer steps in approving the loan. Here is how the loan process works: The lender takes application from the borrower. A credit report is ordered, along with a preliminary title report. An appraisal is ordered. Employment confirmations are sent out. Then, after all of this is completed, an adequate appraisal, a committee approves or disapproves the loan request.

Under VA and FHA conditions an additional step or two is required. Specifically, an inspector will check out the encumbered house to be sure it meets VA and FHA standards. If it doesn't, the seller must make repairs to meet these standards before the loan can be issued. (This requirement is to keep the homebuyer from buying a substandard home, which in turn will protect the lender as well.)

As you can see, with all this bureaucratic red tape involved in processing a loan, it's understandable how the process can get bogged down. These delays are very frustrating to prospective borrowers; however, these hassles can easily be overcome by the smart investor who uses the ease, the simplicity, and the more profitable method of loan assumption.

A Note to the Reader

See the section on Wrap-Around Mortgage in Chapter 16, Creative Financing Strategies, to learn profit techniques available on assumable loans.

7 30-YEAR FIXED-RATE LOAN

Traditionally, the 30-year fixed-rate loan has been the most popular form of home financing. It features a constant (fixed) rate of interest over the life of the loan and fully amortizes (pays off) by maturity the entire loan balance. However, because of rising interest rates institutional lenders in the past have suffered losses on these fixed-rate notes. It was the adjustable-rate loan that emerged to offset this risk to lenders.

THE 30-YEAR FIXED-RATE LOAN AT A GLANCE

- Beginning interest rate is higher than ARM, but it never changes
- Monthly payments remain the same and fully amortize the loan by maturity

Special Conventional Terms
If the loan is "conventional" (not a VA or FHA mortgage), the following conditions are also present:

- Prepayment penalty
- Higher down payment required
- Maximum loan amount: $168,700
- Conventional fixed-rate loans are usually not assumable

The following material further describes each of the above items.

Interest Rate Is Constant
This predictability is the greatest advantage of the fixed-rate over the adjustable-rate loan. The higher initial rate as compared to the ARM is

the premium paid the lender for the advantage of having a fixed rate of interest. (The ARM shifts the unpredictable future rate of interest from lender to the borrower.)

Equal Monthly Payments

Because the interest rate remains constant, monthly payments for principal and interest remain the same. Furthermore, since the 30-year fixed-rate loan is fully amortized, the entire debt is paid off at maturity without owing a balloon.

Special Conventional Terms

A conventional loan usually has a prepayment penalty clause, which means six months' interest is due the lender as a penalty for prematurely paying off the loan. (VA and FHA loans do not have prepayment penalty clauses written into their notes.)

Higher Down Payment Required. Conventional loans require a minimum of 5 percent cash as a down payment, as compared to no money down on VA loans and about 5 percent for FHA loans. In addition, if the down payment is less than 20 percent (considered standard for a conventional loan), then mortgage insurance has to be paid (about 0.5 percent monthly) by the borrower on the unpaid loan balance.

$168,700 Maximum Loan Amount. The maximum conventional loan amount is $168,700, although larger loans are available with different terms. (Requirements of the secondary mortgage market make it necessary to have this limit.)

No Assumability. Conventional fixed-rate loans, in most cases, are not assumable. This is very important if you plan to sell your property because it means that your buyer will have to create new financing. (This inflexibility with severely inhibit the sale of your property. On the other hand, assumable financing adds flexibility because, as the seller, you have built-in financing without the necessity of new financing in order to sell your property.)

PROS AND CONS

In today's mortgage market about half of the loans issued have a fixed rate; the remainder are adjustable rate. Institutional lenders prefer the adjustable-rate over the fixed-rate mortgage, because under a long-term fixed-rate mortgage the lender incurs all the risk of unpredictable market interest rates. The ARM shifts the risk of unpredictable future interest rates to the borrower by periodically adjusting the rate as changes in the market rate occur.

Thus, the greatest advantage of the fixed-rate loan to the borrower is its predictability: The interest rate and loan payment are fixed over the term of the loan. If market interest rates rise after the loan is issued, the borrower will benefit in lower costs from having a loan at a rate below market rates. Conversely, if market interest rates drop after loan issuance, the borrower is faced with the fact that he has contracted for a loan above market interest rates. However, the borrower does have the option of refinancing (at additional costs) the existing loan at the lower market interest rate.

Essentially, there are two other advantages to the 30-year fixed rate loan. The first is that substantial tax deductions for the cost of interest are available, especially in the early years of the loan, because most of the payment is applied to interest in the early years. The other advantage, if the lender allows it, is that you could prepay the principal (pay more than the minimum required), allowing you to shorten the term of the loan. (Note: the "or more" clause in a note allows the borrower to pay more without penalty.)

There are certain disadvantages associated with the fixed-rate loan as well.

Disadvantages

First, in the beginning the interest rate charged on the fix-rate mortgage is higher than the ARM. (This is the premium you pay the lender to have the advantage of a fixed rate when market rates are always changing.)

Second, you have to take into consideration that equity accumulation under the 30-year amortization schedule is very slow, especially compared to the 15-year schedule. (See the comparison of 15- and 30-year equity accumulation in Table 8.1 in the next chapter.)

The third disadvantage is that a conventional loan is likely to have a prepayment penalty written into it. This means six months' interest is due the lender for premature payoff of a loan the lender might otherwise receive income on for 30 years.

Finally, if you sell your home, the buyer cannot assume your loan since a 30-year conventional fixed-rate mortgage is usually not assumable.

8 15-YEAR FIXED-RATE LOAN

Considered a shortcut to home ownership, this distant cousin of the 30-year fixed-rate loan offers a slightly lower interest rate and faster principal payoff than its relative.

15-YEAR FIXED-RATE LOAN AT A GLANCE

- Interest rate is fixed for 15 years
- Rate of interest is slightly less than a 30-year loan
- Loan payments remain the same over term

Special Conventional Terms

- Prepayment penalty
- Maximum loan amount: $168,700
- Conventional loans are usually not assumable.

PROS AND CONS

The 15-year fixed-rate loan is ideal for those who can afford the higher monthly payments. These higher monthly payments result in a savings of tens of thousands of dollars in interest compared to a 30-year payoff (see Table 8.1). And don't forget, you will also enjoy the satisfaction of owning your home, free and clear, in half the time it takes with 30-year mortgage.

Faster Principal Payoff

As with all fully amortized loans, the initial mortgage payments are mostly for interest; this portion gradually becomes less as the loan pays down. But, with a shorter-term loan such as the 15-year, a larger

Table 8.1 Comparing Accumulated Equity and Interest Paid on 15- and 30-Year Loans
(Contract interest rate of 10 percent; loan amount $70,000)

	15-Year Accumulated		30-Year Accumulated	
Time	Interest Paid	Equity Earned	Interest Paid	Equity Earned
After 5 yrs	$32,044	$13,090	$34,479	$2380
After 15 yrs	65,401	70,000	97,766	12,810
After 30 yrs	—	—	151,152	70,000

amount of principal is paid (especially in the beginning). Table 8.1 shows accumulated equity after five years.

You also save on the cost of interest. The shorter term of the 15-year mortgage is where most of the savings occur; although the lower rate of interest is also helpful.

Table 8.2 shows required monthly principal and interest payments for a $70,000 loan at various selected rates of interest at both 15 and 30 years. Don't forget that 15-year loans require a slightly lower rate of interest (perhaps 0.5 percent) than 30-year loans.

LOOKING TO REDUCE THE COST OF DEBT

To reduce the overall cost of borrowing, consider the advantage of a 15-year mortgage. As compared to a 30-year fixed-rate mortgage, it usually carries a slightly lower rate and the shorter term further reduces lifetime interest costs. However, it locks the borrower into a higher payment schedule that may place an unacceptable strain on a budget.

Voluntary Payments of Principal

Consider making overpayments on the mortgage. If you systematically overpay your mortgage each month, even by a modest amount, this will shorten its life significantly and drastically reduce the total interest costs.

Research has shown that paying an extra $25 a month on a $100,000, 10.25 percent, 30-year fixed-rate mortgage would take four years off the loan's lifespan and save the borrower $38,559 in interest. Over-

Table 8.2 Comparison of 15- and 30-Year Loans at Selected Rates of Interest (Loan Amount $70,000)

Interest Rate (%)	Payment Required 15-Year Loan	Payment Required 30-Year Loan
8.0	669	514
8.5	689	538
9.0	710	563
9.5	731	589
10.0	752	614
10.5	774	640
11.0	796	667
12.0	840	720
13.0	886	774
14.0	932	829
15.0	980	885

paying by $100 a month has dramatic saving benefits: on the same loan, savings would amount to $94,389 and the term would be reduced to 19 years.

Other variations produce similar results. There is a biweekly mortgage that consists of a payment every two weeks instead of once a month. Because paying every two weeks results in 26 payments a year, there is substantial savings of interest and time of payoff.

None of these plans increases the borrower's annual outlays very much. Normally, the monthly payment on a $100,000, 10.25 percent mortgage is $896, or an annual outlay of $10,752. That's quite a hunk of change for most families; however, if you add another $100 per month it would push the payment to almost $1000 per month and a total annual outlay of $11,952.

These rapid paydowns give borrowers the ability to manage debt better than a slower amortizing loan. With the speedier payoff of the home loan, the borrower is quicker at building up equity in the home. Later, this equity can be tapped with a home equity loan.

Homeowners are well advised to examine their financial needs carefully before hastening to pay off their mortgages. The extra payments could be put in savings to fund future educational or medical costs. Retrieving the equity later could be more expensive if rates rise.

A rule of thumb is in order here. A home mortgage interest rate becomes expensive at 10 percent. Anything less than 10 percent is considered a favorable mortgage rate; a rate of 10 percent or more is considered expensive or unfavorable. For now, this gauge of value works. What the future will hold depends on the volatility of interest rate movement. Those loans below 10 percent are valuable, it's cheap money. Keep the cheap money. Should hyperinflationary times return, future mortgage payments will be made with cheaper dollars, benefiting the borrower. If interest rates rise, the homeowner can hang on to the below-market-rate loan. And finally, if interest rates plunge, the homeowner has the option to refinance.

9 ADJUSTABLE-RATE MORTGAGE

Adjustable-rate mortgages (ARMs)—in some parts of the country referred to as *variable-rate mortgages* (VRMs)—evolved to meet the needs of lenders and borrowers alike. This type of mortgage adjusts monthly loan payments according to changes in certain indexes. The homebuyer gets a reduced initial rate of interest as compared to a similar fixed-rate mortgage, but, in exchange, is obligated to take on the risk that interest rates will rise in the future.

Before any more is said, let's take a brief look at some of the futures of the ARM.

ARM AT A GLANCE

- Rate of interest fluctuates up or down depending on the rate index
- Initial rate of interest is more favorable than a fixed rate; increases over term of loan are limited
- Borrower's monthly payment will rise or fall over term, to a limited extent
- Buyer's qualify at the second year rate, which usually means a smaller annual income is needed than for a fixed-rate loan.
- Most ARMs are assumable.

Half a century ago the home loan system in the United States thrived on the fixed-rate mortgage. Back then, about the only choice in loan selection was the length of time you needed to pay it off. Today there is a wide variety of real estate financing available, but the most important decision the borrower is confronted with is whether to select the adjustable- or fixed-rate mortgage. Both forms have substantial advantages as well as disadvantages that should be considered.

From the 1930s to just before 1980, interest rates were relatively stable, and fixed-rate loans served the needs of homebuyers and mortgage lenders alike. Then came the hyperinflationary times of the early 1980s when interest rates were at their highest and many families were priced out of the home market. Another result was that long-term mortgage lenders began losing money and became reluctant to underwrite fixed-rate loans. Thus, the emergence of the ARM in an attempt to resolve the question of what the future will hold for interest rates.

These adjustable loans do carry a certain amount of risk. If the rate goes up and stays up for several years, the borrower will have to pay for the painful results in higher loan payments. On the other hand, if rates decline after loan origination, the borrower will benefit from reduced loan payments.

COMPARING THE ARM WITH FIXED-RATE

Table 9.1 shows the annual payments over the first five years on a 10.5 percent fixed-rate mortgage for $70,000 amortized over 30 years.

By comparison, Table 9.2 illustrates the ARM under the worst-case scenario, wherein the worst possible conditions occur and the interest rate is adjusted upward at its maximum permissible change. This particular example increases 2 percent annually with a 5 percent lifetime cap. Again, the amount borrowed is $70,000 over a term of 30 years.

From Table 9.2, the total of annual payments for five years is $40,760 compared to $38,420 in Table 9.1. At the four-year mark total payments for both mortgages are most nearly equal.

Table 9.1 Fixed-Rate Mortgage

Year	Interest Rate (%)	Annual Total of Payments
1	10.5	$7684
2	10.5	7684
3	10.5	7684
4	10.5	7684
5	10.5	7684

Table 9.2 Adjustable-Rate Mortgage

Year	Interest Rate (%)	Annual Total of Payments
1	8	$6164
2	10	7372
3	12	8640
4	13	9292
5	13	9292

Bear in mind that Table 9.2 only illustrates the worst conditions. Since we don't actually know what will happen in the future, it is safe to say that it is unlikely the worst conditions will, in fact, occur. Thus, we can assume that interest rates will rise moderately, in which case we can form the following conclusions in comparing the ARM with the fixed-rate mortgage:

- In the short term (four years or less) ARMs cost less
- At a term of four years the forms are about equal
- Over the long term (more than four years) the fixed-rate mortgage will cost less

HOW ARMs WORK

The adjustable-rate mortgage's interest rate is allowed to change (along with your monthly payment) every one, three, or five years. The period from one rate change to the next is referred to as the *adjustment period*. Thus, a mortgage with an adjustment period of one year is called a *one-year ARM*.

Rate Change Limits

The interest rate on an ARM is tied to an index. When the index rate moves up or down, so do your payments at the time of adjustment. There are limits, however, on how much your interest rate can change at any one time and over the life of the mortgage. The interest rate change is limited to a maximum of 2 percent during each adjustment period and an overall cap is placed on the interest increase.

Most lenders use indexes tied to some easily monitored rate, such as the U.S. Treasury securities rate. Then the lender applies a margin to the index used.

Margin

The *margin* is a certain amount added to the index rate to give the rate of interest to be charged. A margin is applied to all ARM's and usually varies among lenders.

One lender may charge the Treasury index plus a margin of 2 percent, whereas another lender may use the same index plus a margin of 3 percent. Thus, after your first period of adjustment, one lender's offering would be 1 percent cheaper, based on the amount of margin applied. Tables 9.3 and 9.4 illustrate the difference in margins and how they affect your monthly payment. The $53 difference in the monthly payments shown in the tables amounts to $19,080 over the life of the loan.

Margins are an integral part of competitive pricing of mortgages and reflect the lender's cost of doing business and resulting profit.

The margin used, the index preferred, and the choice of adjustment periods are the essential subjects to discuss when shopping for a mortgage. Besides comparing margins among lenders, you also have some options on how often your rate will be adjusted. Keep in mind however, that lenders will charge a higher rate for longer adjustment periods.

Table 9.3 Margin Application Using a 2 Percent Margin

One-year Treasury index	9%
Margin	+2%
Mortgage interest rate*	11%

*Monthly principal and interest at 11 percent is $667 (based on a $70,000 loan for 30 years).

Table 9.4 Margin Application Using a 3 Percent Margin

One-year Treasury index	9%
Margin	+3%
Mortgage interest rate*	12%

*Monthly principal and interest at 12 percent is $720 on a $70,000 loan for 30 years.
$720 − $667 = $53 difference per month.

Safeguard Features

Many lenders offer certain *caps*, or specified limits on how much rates, or monthly payments, can increase in any adjustment period or over the term of the loan. Most ARMs have both payment caps and interest rate caps.

Payment Caps. A *payment cap* sets a ceiling on how much your monthly payments can increase in any one year. As an example, suppose you have a $70,000, one-year ARM with a 7.5 percent payment cap and market interest rates rise by 2.5 percent:

Mortgage interest rate for the first year	9%
Monthly payment (P&I)	$563
Mortgage interest rate for the second year	11.5%
Monthly payment (P&I) without payment cap (an increase of 23%)	$693
Monthly payment (P&I) with payment cap (an increase of 7.5%)	$605

$693 less $605 is a difference of $88 per month.

The payment cap limits the increase in your monthly payments. Thus, in the above example, you are protected from an additional $88 increase in your monthly payments. However, the $88 cannot be considered a savings; in fact it is deferred interest, often referred to as *negative amortization*. Your lender adds this $88 each month to the unpaid balance on your loan. Although it would be unwise to defer interest indefinitely, it can be a useful tactic in the beginning when one's income is low and expected to increase later on.

In any event, a payment cap provision protects the borrower from what is termed *payment shock*, that is, a sudden order by your lender to pay excessively more.

Interest Rate Caps. *Interest rate caps* limit the increases in the interest rate itself. These caps come in two varieties:

- Caps that limit the amount of increase in interest rate from one adjustment period to the next.
- Caps that limit the amount of increase in interest rate over the life of the loan.

These caps act to insure the borrower and, like other forms of insurance, you have to pay to get them. How much depends on each particular mortgage situation. The additional cost of caps, usually not more than half of 1 percent (0.5%), can be included in the monthly payment.

The following example illustrates the application of an interest rate cap from one adjustment period to another for a $70,000, one-year ARM limited to a 2 percent cap on changes in the interest rate per adjustment period. In this example, interest rates rise 3 percent, but the interest rate for the mortgage is limited to a 2 percent rise. Here's how it works:

Mortgage interest rate, first year	9%
Monthly payment	$563
Mortgage interest rate, second year	11%
Monthly payment with interest rate cap (an increase of 18%)	$667
Monthly payment without interest rate cap (an increase of 28%)	$720

Interest rate caps may also be applied to the overall life of the loan, such as a limit of 5 percent change over the entire term. In the following example, the interest rate is limited to a 2 percent increase per adjustment period, not to exceed 5 percent over the term of the loan. This example illustrates the the worst-case scenario for your adjustable-rate mortgage; that is, the interest rate on your mortgage increases at its maximum permissible rate after issuance.

The difference between $830 and $563 is $267. Over the life of the mortgage that amounts to more than $80,000. Of course, this is expecting the worst from an unpredictable future.

Mortgage interest rate, first year	9%
Monthly payment	$563
Mortgage interest rate, second year	11%
Monthly payment with 2% annual interest rate cap	$667
Mortgage interest rate, third year	13%
Monthly payment with 2% annual interest rate cap	$774
Mortgage interest rate, fourth year	14%
Monthly payment with 5% overall interest rate life cap	$830

You are now aware that the payments on ARMs can move up or down depending on interest rates in the economy. From the example, the worst that can possibly happen on an average loan, in this case $70,000, is a maximum increase in payments of $267.

But what happens if interest rates stay the same or decline? If interest rates stay the same, then as a rule your payments will stay the same. If they decline, your payment will likewise decline, as they have in the recent past. In June, 1982, the interest rate on a one-year ARM was 16 percent; in June, 1983, the rate declined to 12 percent. This means that the monthly payment on the $70,000 loan would have been reduced from $942 to $720.

There is much to consider when choosing an ARM. Remember that lending is a highly competitive business and lenders in your area may offer different features on ARMs in an attempt to compete for your business.

SUMMARY

The adjustable-rate mortgage is a relatively new solution for lenders to overcome the long-term unpredictability in today's economic climate. With the ARM, lenders shift to the borrower the risk that interest rates will rise in the future. With all the various options available for the ARM, and the tremendous savings that derive from the right selection, it is wise to become informed about the particulars of the ARM.

You should examine all the options from more than one lender and select the one that is best for you. For example, one lender may combine a number of features on one mortgage, such as an overall cap on the term interest rate, payment caps, and a cap on the amount of interest that can be deferred. Another lender may offer a lower initial rate of interest with a higher margin and interest rate caps.

Most of all you should consider that over the short term (four years or less), the ARM will be less expensive than a fixed-rate mortgage. Obviously, this information is very helpful once you determine how long you plan on maintaining the mortgage.

Also, consider that a mortgage with built-in payment increases might be feasible if you can realistically expect your future income to increase. On the other hand, this type of loan could lead to financial disaster if your income is apt to stay the same, or decrease, in the next few years.

Finally, you should be prepared to ask lenders certain questions about ARMs. The following are important factors about ARMs that you should discuss with lenders:

- How much margin is applied and what index is used for determining mortgage interest rate?
- What will happen to my mortgage payments if interest rates rise, decline, or stay the same?
- How often will monthly payments be adjusted?
- What type of caps are available for my protection?

In conclusion, there is a national trend toward uniform standards on ARMs, thus making it less complicated for the consumer to select the right loan. When you're out shopping for a real estate loan, don't be bashful—ask a lot of questions and compare what lenders have to offer. Remember, a difference of a few points can result in paying $30,000 or more too much in interest charges over the life of the average mortgage.

QUESTIONS AND ANSWERS ABOUT ARMs

Why is an adjustable-rate mortgage affordable to more people?

In qualifying for a loan, lenders look at the portion of your income that is available to make your mortgage payment. Many lenders require that portion for monthly mortgage payments (that is, principal, interest, taxes, and insurance) should not exceed 25 to 28 percent of a borrower's gross monthly income.

With a 28 percent standard and an average $100 a month for taxes and insurance, it takes an average gross annual income of $35,126 to qualify for a $70,000 fixed-rate mortgage at 12 percent but only $30,643 income for an ARM at 10 percent.

What's the difference between adjustable-rate and fixed-rate mortgage?

With a fixed-rate mortgage the rate of interest remains the same over the term of the loan. Therefore, your payment for principal and interest remains constant over the life of the loan. With the ARM the interest rate and monthly payment do change; they can go up or down depending on what market rates do. The initial ARM interest rate is commonly lower than a fixed-rate mortgage; however, if market rates go up, so does your monthly payment. Consequently, you will initially pay less for your mortgage loan, but you incur the risk that market rates will increase in the future.

Of course, the borrower's primary concern is that market rates will rise, but if rates fall as they did in 1983, the mortgage payment will decline.

What are the benefits of an ARM?

Compared to the fixed-rate mortgage, the ARM can be cheaper overall if you plan to sell your home in four years or less, In addition, ARMs usually are initiated at 2 points below that of fixed-rate mortgages. And, ARMs have lower income requirements, which allow more buyers to qualify for housing.

10 CONVERTIBLE ARM

The latest "special" in innovative financing is the adjustable-rate mortgage that can be converted to a fixed-rate loan. It is special, in particular, because it's the hybrid of the adjustables and fixed rates. It gives you the best of both worlds: the lower initial rates of the ARM and the option to lock in a fixed rate at some future time.

CONVERTIBLE ARM AT A GLANCE

- Rate of interest fluctuates; however, borrower can lock in a fixed rate when the time of convertibility is right.
- Slightly higher interest rate than the ARM, plus a conversion fee. (You pay for the right to have a valuable option.)
- When you convert to a fixed rate on your adjustment period anniversary date, the rate is usually one-quarter percentage point higher than the going rate of your lender's fixed-rate mortgage.
- Assumability was undetermined at the time of this writing. Please check with your lender.
- This type of loan is ideal for those who (1) like to take advantage of lower initial interest rates and fear the results of future rising rates and (2) are likely to be selling the newly financed home within five years.

PROS AND CONS

Especially for those homebuyers who expect to sell within five years, convertible ARMs being a certain predictability to mortgage needs. (The biggest disadvantage of standard ARMs is the unpredictability of the future interest.) Most convertibles allow you to switch from an adjustable rate to a fixed rate on the anniversary dates of the loan closing, generally limited to a three to five year conversion period. If you never convert, then your mortgage loan continues as a typical ARM with a cap on rate increases, limited to an overall 5 point increase over the term.

Cost of conversion varies with each lender, but generally it's in a range of $250 to $1000. This can be a substantial savings compared to refinancing, which usually costs between $1500 and $2000.

Convertible loan rates are usually lower than fixed-rate loans but slightly higher than similar ARMs without convertibility. The cost of loan origination is about the same as the ARM; nevertheless, be prepared to pay a premium to the lender (in addition to the conversion fee) for the right of convertibility.

SUMMARY

The convertible ARM is, by far, the loan to select when you have to originate new financing. As mentioned above, it offers you the best of both worlds: the lower initial rate of the standard ARM and the ability to grab a fixed rate on certain specified dates. This type of loan becomes extremely valuable to the borrower when the market interest rate falls below the rate being paid; then the borrower can convert and lock into a low-interest rate. This converted rate will stay the same until the mortgage loan matures at term's end.

11 FHA FINANCING

The Federal Housing Administration (FHA), a division of the U.S. Department of Housing and Urban Development (HUD), provides mortgage insurance to private institutional lenders to facilitate home ownership and the construction and financing of housing.

By insuring lenders against loss, the FHA encourages them to invest capital in the home mortgage market. Under FHA insurance programs lenders can make loans for up to 97 percent of property value and for terms of up to 30 years.

FHA FINANCING AT A GLANCE

- Down payment is about 5 percent, substantially less than conventional financing
- Interest rate is about 1 percent below that of conventional financing.
- Maximum loan amount, $101,250
- No prepayment penalty
- FHA loans are assumable, with certain exceptions

PROS AND CONS

In addition to the advantage of lower interest rates and down payment requirements, FHA loans are also assumable, with two important exceptions. FHA-insured loans issued on or after December 1, 1986, require that the assumptor's credit be reviewed if the loan being assumed is less than two years old and originated after this date (one year if owner occupied). The second exception says that if the original mortgagor does not get a release from the mortgage, the buyer and seller will have joint liability for five years after the assumption. This provision also applies to all mortgages issued on or after December 1, 1986.

FHA loans may be prepaid without penalty; however, homeowners may be liable for one month's interest if a 30-day notice of intent to prepay is not submitted to the lender servicing the mortgage.

In addition, FHA-insured homeowners threatened with foreclosure due to circumstances beyond their control, such as job loss, death, or illness in the family, may apply for assignment of the mortgage to HUD which, if it accepts assignment, takes over the mortgage and adjusts the mortgage payments for a period of time until the homeowner can resume the financial obligation.

About the only negative thing to buying a home under one of many FHA programs is the bureaucratic red tape involved. As mentioned earlier, FHA loans can take 60 to 90 days or more to close.

The following are FHA requirements under the most popular available program, Title II, Section 203(b). Additional programs are also available and will be described later in this chapter.

ONE- TO FOUR-FAMILY DWELLINGS (SECTION 203 [b])

This program is meant to facilitate the financing of one- to four-family dwellings, either proposed, under construction, or existing.

Applicant Eligibility

Any person able to meet the cash investment, the mortgage payments, and the credit requirements is eligible for a FHA-insured loan.

Qualification

FHA guidelines require a limit of about 28 percent of the borrower's gross monthly income for payment of principal, interest, taxes, and insurance.

Loan Terms

The maximum loan is $101,250 on single-family dwellings. Down payment stipulations require the FHA buyer to place 3 percent down on the first $25,000 of the loan and 5 percent on the remaining amount borrowed when the property is owner occupied.

The maximum FHA loan may not exceed 75 percent of the appraised value when it is to nonresident owners (investors).

The maximum term is 30 years or 75 percent of the existing economic life of the property, whichever is less. If the buyer does not qualify at a term of 30 years, it may be increased to 35 years.

Interest rates are adjusted by the FHA Commissioner as necessary.

Down Payment

The down payment on new FHA loans must be in cash or other assets including existing mortgages or deeds of trust. It is prohibited to attain secondary financing for the down payment, unless a buyer is 62 years of age or older. Such a person may borrow the down payment and closing costs from a person or corporation approved by the FHA but not a broker or lending institution. The buyer must still meet the qualifications for monthly payments of the supplementary loan.

Mortgage Insurance

The FHA charges the borrower 0.5 percent per annum premium on the average outstanding loan balance to insure the lender against loss. (Recent changes require the FHA to charge 3.8 percent of the loan proceeds up front for this insurance which can either be paid in cash or financed over the term.)

Impounds

The FHA requires lenders to collect from the borrower prorated funds to cover real estate taxes and hazard insurance premiums. Lenders will not make loans unless they determine that these liabilities will be paid when due. Thus, a prorated amount for these liabilities is added to the monthly principal and interest payment.

OTHER FHA PROGRAMS AVAILABLE

Home Ownership Assistance for Low- and Moderate-Income Families (Section 235)

This program, which is to be terminated in October, 1989, provides mortgage insurance and interest subsidy for low- and moderate-income homebuyers who purchase new homes that meet HUD standards. HUD insures mortgages and makes monthly payments to lenders to reduce interest to as low as 4 percent. The homeowner must contribute 20 percent of adjusted income to monthly mortgage payments and make a down payment of 3 percent of the cost of acquisition. Mortgage limits are $40,000 ($47,500 for homes for five or more persons) and, in high-cost areas, $47,500 ($55,000 for homes for five or more persons). The income limit for initial eligibility is 95 percent of the area median income for a family of four and the sales price may not exceed 120 percent of the mortgage limit.

Eligibility. A homebuyer's adjusted family income may not exceed a certain percentage of local median income, depending upon family size. There is no restriction on assets.

Home Ownership Assistance for Low- and Moderate-Income Families (Section 221[d][2]

This program provides mortgage insurance to encourage home ownership for low- and moderate-income families, especially those displaced by urban renewel.

This HUD program insures lenders against loss on mortgage loans to finance the purchase, construction, or rehabilitation of low-cost, one- to four-family housing. Maximum insurable loans for an owner-occupant are $31,000 for a single-family home (up to $36,000 in high-cost areas). For a larger family (five or more persons), the limits are $36,000 or up to $42,000 in high-cost areas. Higher mortgage limits apply to two- and four-family housing.

Eligibility. Anyone may apply; displaced households qualify for special terms.

Housing in Declining Neighborhoods (Section 223[e])

This program provides mortgage insurance to purchase or rehabilitate housing in older, declining urban areas.

In consideration of the need for adequate housing for low- and moderate-income families, HUD insures lenders against loss on mortgage loans to finance the purchase, rehabilitation, or construction of housing in older, declining, but still viable urban areas where conditions are such that normal requirements for mortgage insurance cannot be met. A provision relaxed these requirements but specified that the property must be an acceptable risk. The terms of the loans vary according to the HUD/FHA program under which the mortgage is insured.

Eligibility. Home or project owners who are ineligible for FHA mortgage insurance because the property is located in an older, declining urban area.

Condominium Housing (Section 234)

This program provides mortgage insurance to finance ownership of individual units in multifamily housing projects.

HUD insures mortgages made by private lending institutions for the purchase of individual family units in multifamily housing projects under Section 234(c). Sponsors may also obtain FHA-insured mortgages to finance the construction or rehabilitation of housing projects that they intend to sell as individual condominium units under Section 234(d). A project must contain at least four dwelling units. They may be detached, semi-detached, row, walkup, or elevator structures. Recent changes in legislation permit insuring mortgages on individual units in existing condominiums.

A condominium is defined as joint ownership of common areas and facilities by the separate owners of single dwelling units in the project.

Eligibility. Any qualified profit-motivated or nonprofit sponsor may apply for a blanket mortgage covering the project after conferring with the local HUD-FHA field office. Any credit-worthy person may apply for a mortgage on individual units in a project.

Cooperative Housing (Section 213)

This program provides mortgage insurance to finance cooperative housing projects.

HUD insures mortgages made by private lending institutions on cooperative housing projects of five or more dwelling units to be occupied by members of nonprofit, cooperative ownership housing corporations. These loans may finance new construction; rehabilitation; acquisition; improvement or repair of a project already owned; resale of individual memberships; construction of projects composed of individual family dwellings to be bought by individual members with separate insured mortgages; and construction or rehabilitation of projects that the owners intend to sell to nonprofit cooperatives.

Eligibility. Nonprofit corporations or trusts organized to construct homes for members of the corporation or beneficiaries of the trust are eligible, as are qualified sponsors who intend to sell the project to a nonprofit corporation or trust.

Manufactured (Mobile) Homes (Title I)

This program provides insurance of loans to facilitate financing of manufactured-home purchases, thereby providing alternative lower-cost housing. HUD insures manufactured-home loans by private lending institutions. The maximum amount of loan is $40,500 for either a single or a multisection home, and $54,000 for a manufactured home and a suitably developed lot. The maximum loan term is 20 years and 32 days.

Eligibility. Any person able to make the cash investment, mortgage payments, and credit requirements.

Manufactured-Home Parks (Section 207)

This program provides mortgage insurance to finance construction or rehabilitation of manufactured-home parks consisting of five or more spaces. HUD insures mortgages made by private lending institutions on the entire site. Mortgages are limited to $9000 per individual manufactured-home space within each park. In high-cost areas, this maximum may be increased up to $15,750 per space. The park must be located in an area approved by HUD and market conditions must show a need for such housing.

Eligibility. Investors, builders, developers, cooperatives, and others who meet HUD requirements may apply to an FHA- approved lending institution after conferring with the local HUD office.

Multifamily Rental Housing (Section 207)

HUD will insure mortgages made by private lending institutions to finance the construction or rehabilitation of multifamily rental housing by private or public developers. The project must contain at least five dwelling units. Housing financed under this program, whether in urban or suburban areas, should be able to accommodate families (with or without children) at reasonable rents.

Eligibility. Investors, builders, developers, and others who meet HUD requirements may apply for funds at an FHA-approved lending institution after conferring with the local HUD office. The housing project must be located in an area approved by HUD for rental housing and in which market conditions show a need for such housing.

Existing Multifamily Rental Housing (Section 223[f])

This program provides mortgage insurance to facilitate purchase or refinancing of existing multifamily projects originally financed with or without federal mortgage insurance. Under this program HUD may insure mortgages on existing multifamily projects that do not require substantial rehabilitation. Project must contain at least five units and must be at least three years old.

Eligibility. Investors, builders, developers, and others who meet HUD requirements are eligible.

Multifamily Rental Housing for Low- and Moderate-Income Families (Section 221[d] [3] and [4])

HUD insures mortgages made by private lending institutions to help finance construction or substantial rehabilitation of multifamily (five or more units) rental or cooperative housing for moderate-income or displaced families. Projects in both cases may consist of detached, semi-detached, row, walkup, or elevator structures.

Currently, the principal difference between subsections of the program is that HUD may insure up to 100 percent of total project cost under Section 221(d)(3) for nonprofit and cooperative mortgagors but only up to 90 percent under Section 221(d)(4) irrespective of the type of mortgagor.

Eligibility. Sections 221(d)(3) and 221(d)(4) mortgages may be obtained by public agencies; nonprofit, limited-dividend, or cooperative organizatiaons; and private builders or investors who sell completed projects to such organizations. Additionally, Section 221(d)(4) mortgages may be obtained by profit-motivated sponsors. Tenant occupancy is not restricted by income limits.

Assistance to Nonprofit Sponsors of Low- and Moderate-Income Housing (Section 106)

This program provides technical assistance and loans to sponsors of certain HUD-assisted housing.

The nature of this program is to stimulate the production of housing for low- and moderate-income families. HUD will provide information and technical advice to nonprofit organizations that sponsor such multifamily housing.

HUD also makes interest-free "seed money" loans to nonprofit sponsors or public housing agencies to cover 80 percent of the preliminary development costs. Current HUD regulations limit these loans to nonprofit sponsors of Section 202 housing for the elderly or handicapped. Loans may be used to meet typical project development costs such as surveys and market analyses, site engineering, architectural fees, site option expenses, legal fees, consultant fees, and organization expenses. Loans are made from a revolving Low- and Moderate-Income Sponsor Fund.

Eligibility. Nonprofit sponsors eligible under HUD regulations and public housing agencies.

Rent Supplements (Section 101)

This program provides payments to reduce rents for certain disadvantaged, low-income persons.

HUD may pay rent supplements on behalf of eligible tenants to private owners of multifamily housing insured by the FHA. The payment makes up the difference between 30 percent of tenant's adjusted income and the fair market rent determined by HUD. However, the subsidy may not exceed 70 percent of the HUD-approved rent for the specific unit. HUD may pay the supplements for a maximum term of 40 years.

Eligibility. Private nonprofit, limited dividend, cooperative, or public agency sponsors carrying mortgages insured under the following programs may apply for rent supplements: Sections 221(d)(3), 231, 236, and Section 202. (The basic mortgage insurance vehicle has been the Section 221[d][3], Market Interest Rate program.) Eligible tenants are limited to low-income households that qualify for public housing and are either elderly, handicapped, displaced by government action, victims of national disaster, occupants of substandard housing, or headed by a person serving on active military duty.

Lower-Income Rental Assistance (Section 8)

This program aids low- and very low-income families in obtaining decent, safe, and sanitary housing in private accommodations.

It is the nature of this program for HUD to make up the difference between what a low- and very low-income household can afford and the fair-market rent for an adequate housing unit. Eligible tenants must pay the highest of either 30 percent of adjusted income, 10 percent of gross income, or the portion of welfare assistance designated to meet housing costs. Housing thus subsidized by HUD must meet certain standards of safety and sanitation, and rents for these units must fall within the range of fair-market rents as determined by HUD. This rental assistance may be used in existing housing, in new construction, and in moderately or substantially rehabilitated units.

Eligibility. Project sponsors may be private owners; profit-motivated, nonprofit, or cooperative organizations; public housing agencies; and state housing finance agencies. Very low-income families whose incomes do not exceed 50 percent of the median income for the area are eligible to occupy the assisted units. No more than 5 percent of the available units may be rented to low-income families whose incomes are between 50 percent and 80 percent of median.

Direct Loans for Housing for the Elderly or Handicapped (Section 202)

This program provides long-term direct loans to eligible, private, nonprofit sponsors to finance rental or cooperative housing facilities for occupancy by elderly or handicapped persons. The current interest rate is based on the average rate paid in federal obligations during the preceding fiscal year.

Eligibility. Private, nonprofit sponsors may qualify for loans. Households of one or more persons, the head of which is at least 62 years old or a qualified, nonelderly, handicapped person between the ages of 18 and 62, are eligible to live in the structures.

Mortgage Insurance for Housing for the Elderly (Section 231)

This program provides mortgage insurance to facilitate financing of construction or rehabilitation of rental housing for the elderly or handicapped.

The purpose of this program to assure a supply of rental housing suited to the needs of the elderly or handicapped. HUD insures mortgages made by private lending institutions to build or rehabilitate multifamily projects consisting of eight or more units. HUD may insure up to 100 percent of project cost for nonprofit and public mortgagors, but only up to 90 percent for private mortgagors.

Eligibility. Investors, builders, developers, public bodies, and nonprofit sponsors may qualify for mortgage insurance. All elderly (62 or older) or handicapped persons are eligible to occupy units in a project whose mortgage is insured under this program.

Mortgage and Major Home Improvement Loan Insurance for Urban Renewal Areas (Section 220)

This program provides insured loans used to finance mortgages for housing in urban renewal areas in which concentrated revitalization activities have been undertaken by local government, or to alter, repair, or improve housing in those areas.

HUD uses this program to insure mortgages on new or rehabilitated homes or multifamily structures located in designated urban renewal areas with concentrated programs of code enforcement and neighborhood development. HUD insures supplemental loans to finance improvements that will enhance and preserve salvageable homes and apartments in designated urban renewal areas.

Eligibility. Investors, builders, developers, individual homeowners, and apartment owners.

Home Improvement Loan Insurance (Title I)

This program provides insurance of loans to finance home improvements. HUD will insure loans to finance major and minor improvements, alterations, and repairs of individual homes and nonresidential structures (whether owned or leased). The loans may be up to $17,500 and may extend to 15 years and 32 days. Loans on apartment buildings may be as high as $8750 per unit, but the total for the building may not exceed $43,750 and the term may not exceed 15 years. Loans may also finance new construction for agricultural or nonresidential use. Private lenders process these loans. Loans of not more than $2500 are generally unsecured personal loans.

Eligibility is determined by the lender.

Rehabilitation Mortgage Insurance (Section 203[k])

This program provides mortgage insurance to facilitate rehabilitation of one- to four-family properties.

HUD will insure rehabilitation loans to (1) finance rehabilitation of an existing property; (2) finance rehabilitation and refinancing of the outstanding indebtedness of a property; and (3) finance purchase and rehabilitation of a property. An eligible rehabilitation loan must involve a principal obligation not exceeding the amount allowed under Section 203(b) home mortgage insurance.

Eligibility. Any person able to make the cash investment, mortgage payments, and credit requirements.

Supplemental Loans for Multifamily Projects and Health-Care Facilities (Section 241)

This program provides loan insurance to facilitate financing of improvements to multifamily rental housing and health-care facilities.

HUD will insure loans made by private lending institutions to pay for improvements to apartment projects, nursing homes, hospitals, or group practice facilities that carry HUD-insured mortgages. Projects may also obtain FHA insurance on loans to expand housing opportunities, to provide fire and safety equipment, or to finance energy conservation improvements to conventionally financed projects. Major movable equipment for nursing homes, group practice facilities, or hospitals also may be covered by a mortgage under this program.

Eligibility. Qualified owners of projects and health-care facilities (as specified above).

Single-Family Home Mortgage Coinsurance (Section 244)
This program provides joint mortgage insurance by the federal government and private lenders to facilitate home ownership financing.

HUD offers an additional and optional method of insuring lenders against losses on loans they underwrite to finance the purchase of one- to four-family homes. In return for the right to expedite preliminary processing procedures by performing them himself, the lender assumes responsibility for a portion of the insurance premium. Thus coinsurance is expected to result in faster service to the buyer and to improve the quality of loan origination and servicing.

For borrowers, the program operates just like full insurance programs. The major differences affect the lending institution, which performs the loan underwriting and property disposition function normally carried out by HUD alone.

Eligibility. Any mortgagee approved under the full insurance programs may apply for inclusion in this program. The coinsuring lender assesses the characteristics of the property and the credit qualifications of the borrower and determines whether to make the loan.

Multifamily Housing Coinsurance (Section 244)
This program provides joint mortgage insurance by the federal government and state housing agencies and authorized private lenders to facilitate financing of rental housing.

State housing agencies and authorized private lenders that are approved for participation in the program in effect assume the responsibilities of the HUD field office with respect to underwriting mortgage loans and those responsibilities of an FHA-approved mortgagee.

In exchange for the authority to perform the necessary underwriting, servicing, management, and property disposition functions, approved mortgagees assume responsibility for a portion of any insurance loss on the coinsured mortgage. The lender is allowed to retain a share of the mortgage insurance premiums paid by the owner as compensation for assuming a portion of the insurance risk. The program insures mortgages on the purchase or refinancing of existing multifamily housing projects that are at least three years old and have five or more units.

Eligibility. State housing agencies and authorized private lenders as mortgagee and coinsurer. Nonprofit, limited dividend, and profit-motivated entities are eligible to apply to approved state agencies for loans.

Adjustable-Rate Mortgage (ARM) (Section 251)

This program provides mortgage insurance for adjustable-rate mortgages (ARMs).

Under this HUD-insured mortgage, the interest rate and monthly payment may change during the life of the loan. The initial interest rate, discount points, and the margin are negotiable between the buyer and lender.

The one-year Treasury Constant Maturities is the index used for determining the interest-rate changes. The maximum amount the interest rate may increase or decrease in any one year is 1 percent. Over the life of the loan, the maximum interest rate change is 5 percent from the initial rate charged on the loan.

Lenders are required to disclose to the borrower the nature of the ARM at the time of loan application. In addition, borrowers must be informed at least 30 days in advance of any adjustment to the monthly payment.

Eligibility. All FHA-approved lenders may make adjustable-rate mortgages; credit-worthy applicants who are owner-occupants may qualify for such loans.

12 VA FINANCING

The Veterans Administration (VA) is an independent federal agency created in 1930. The Servicemen's Readjustment Act of 1944 authorized the VA to administer various programs to benefit veterans returning to civilian life. In particular, the veterans home-loan guaranty program offers eligible veterans attractive long-term financing with no money down. In addition, lenders are encouraged to make long-term loans to eligible veterans by provisions guaranteeing the lender against loss.

VA FINANCING AT A GLANCE

- No down payment required on loans up to $144,000
- 5 percent down on mobile homes
- Fixed rate of interest, usually 1 point lower than conventional loans
- No prepayment penalty
- Are fully assumable unless closed on or after March 1, 1988.

PROS AND CONS

VA loans offer the eligible veteran notable advantages over conventional forms of financing. In particular, no down payment is required on the first $144,000 borrowed (although 5 percent is required for mobile home loans). The veteran-buyer is required to make a 25 percent down payment for amounts borrowed in excess of $144,000, or if required by the lender when the purchase price is more than the appraised value. Also, a small down payment is required by the lender when the loan is made under the graduated payment form of mortgage loan. Another favorable feature is a fixed rate of interest at below market interest rates. Veteran-buyers are also informed of the property's value through an independent appraisal.

The following are additional features of VA financing:

- Limitation on closing costs
- Favorable repayment terms (long amortization)
- Right to repay early without penalty (lenders may require a partial payment of $100 or one monthly installment, whichever is less)
- An assumable mortgage by a subsequent buyer without qualification (see the note at the end of this chapter)
- For houses appraised by the VA prior to construction, inspections at appropriate stages of construction assure compliance with the approved plans, and there is a one-year warranty to the buyer from the builder that the house is built in conformity with the approved plans and specifications
- Leniency extended to worthy VA homeowners who experience temporary financial difficulty.

About the only disadvantage to VA financing is that they are cumbersome to originate. Like FHA loans, they can take 60 to 90 days or more to close.

VA LOAN REQUIREMENTS

To get a VA loan, the law requires that:

- You must be an eligible veteran who has available home loan entitlement.
- You must occupy or intend to occupy the property as your home within a reasonable period of time after closing.
- You must have enough income to make payments on the new loan, cover the costs of home ownership, take care of other financial obligations, and still have enough income left over for family support (a spouse's income is considered in the same manner as the veteran's).
- You must have a good credit history.

LOAN GUARANTY

VA-guaranteed loans are made by private lenders, such as savings and loans, banks, or mortgage companies. To get a loan, you apply directly to the lender. The guaranty means the lender is protected against loss if you or a subsequent owner fail to repay the loan. If the lender does take a loss, the VA must pay the guaranty to the lender, and the amount paid by the VA must be repaid by you.

Currently there is no limitation on the amount of a loan eligible for a VA loan guaranty. However, there is a restriction on the amount of guaranty that can be issued. The maximum guaranty for a loan to finance the purchase of a dwelling is $36,000, including construction or alteration costs of the dwelling. Generally, most lenders who fund VA loans will lend, with no money down payment required, up to four times the amount of the guaranty. Therefore, $144,000 ($36,000 × 4) is the current maximum loan amount available with no down payment, In addition, the same guaranty is authorized to refinance existing liens of record in owner-occupied homes by eligible veterans.

The VA will also make a loan directly to veterans, but only to supplement a grant to get a specially adapted home for certain eligible veterans who have permanent and total service-connected disability (ies). See VA Pamphlet 26-69-1 for information concerning specially adapted housing grants.

ELIGIBILITY

You are eligible for VA financing if your service falls within any of the following categories:

Wartime Service. If you served any time during the following periods: World War II (September 16, 1940 to July 25, 1947); Korean Conflict (June 27, 1950 to January 31, 1955); or Vietnam Era (August 5, 1964 to May 7, 1975).

You must have served at least 90 days on active duty and been discharged or released under other than dishonorable conditions. If you served less than 90 days, you may be eligible if discharged because of a service-connected disability.

Peacetime Service. If your service fell entirely within any one of the following periods: July 26, 1947, to June 26, 1950; February 1, 1955, to August 4, 1964; or May 8, 1975, to September 7, 1980 (if enlisted personnel) or to October 16, 1981 (if officer).

You must have served at least 181 days of continuous active duty and been discharged or released under conditions other than dishonorable. If you served less than 181 days, you may be eligible if discharged because of a service-connected disability.

Service after September 7, 1980 (enlisted), or October 16, 1981 (officer). If you were separated from service which began after these dates, you must have: (1) completed 24 months of continuous active duty or the full period (at least 181 days) for which you were called or ordered to active duty and been discharged or released under conditions other than dishonorable; or (2) completed at least 181 days of active duty with a hardship discharge, a discharge for the convenience of the government, or been determined to have a compensable service-connected disability; or (3) been discharged for a service-connected disability.

Active Duty Service Personnel. If you are now on active duty, you are eligible after having served on continuous active status for at least 181 days, regardless of when your service began.

Other Types of Service. (1) Certain United States citizens who served in the armed forces of a government allied with the United States in World War II. (2) Unmarried surviving spouses of the above-described eligible persons who died as the result of service or service-connected injuries (children of deceased veterans are not eligible). (3) The spouse of any member of the armed forces serving on active duty who is listed as missing in action or is a prisoner of war and has been so listed for a total of more than 90 days. (4) Individuals with service in certain other organizations, services, programs, and schools may also be eligible. Questions about whether this service qualifies for home loan benefits should be referred to the Loan Guaranty Division of the nearest VA regional office.

Obtaining a Certificate of Eligibility

A veteran may apply for a Certificate of Eligibility at any regional VA office. This request should be accompanied by discharge papers (Form DD-214) or evidence of current active duty status. If you are now on active duty and have not been previously discharged from active duty service, you must submit a statement of service on military letterhead, signed by the adjutant, personnel officer, or commander of your unit or higher headquarters. The statement must include date of entry on active duty and the duration of any time lost.

BUYER QUALIFICATION

VA guidelines recommend a limit of 25 to 28 percent of the gross monthly income for total principal and interest payments. The following guideline for buyer qualification is generally used by those lenders who fund VA loans: The monthly income of both husband and wife less their monthly debt payments should equal four times the total monthly payment of the purchased home. The veteran's job stability and credit worthiness are considered along with present and anticipated income. Overtime pay is not taken into account for long-term projections to meet loan payments but is considered against short-term obligations. The VA does not accept cosigners or comortgagors.

APPRAISED VALUE

Once the eligible veteran locates the property that will accommodate VA financing, the VA will appraise the property and issue a Certificate of Reasonable Value (CRV). The amount of the loan guaranteed cannot exceed the CRV, including construction, alteration, or repairs.

EXISTING LOANS

When a veteran is still liable for a previous VA loan (may still own a home or has allowed a new buyer to assume the existing mortgage), the following method is used to compute the maximum VA loan the lender will make on a new home, based on the veteran's remaining entitlement.

The maximum loan is the equivalent entitlement plus 75 percent of the CRV or the purchase price, whichever is less. For example, assume a veteran bought a home in 1968 using the VA entitlement. (The maximum VA loan guaranty in 1968 was $12,500.) In 1979 that same veteran decided to rent the home and purchase a new home for $80,000 with a CRV equal to the purchase price. What is the maximum VA loan obtainable and how much of a down payment is needed to finance the new home?

Maximum loan guaranty in 1979	$25,000
Less maximum loan guaranty in 1968	−12,500
Remaining veteran entitlement	12,500
Plus 75% of the $80,000 CRV	60,000
Equals maximum loan attainable	$72,500

Therefore, at a purchase price of $80,000 the veteran would need a cash down payment of $7,500 in 1979. Today the veteran wouldn't need a down payment because the guaranty has been raised to $36,000. Hence, the veteran's remaining entitlement would be: $36,000 − $12,500 = $23,500 × 4 = $94,000.

The VA permits entire restoration of a veteran's full entitlement of the current maximum guarantee of $36,000 if the property has been sold and the previous loan has been paid in full. The veteran will also receive full entitlement should the property be sold to another veteran who assumes the existing VA loan with release of liability and agrees to use his/her own entitlement.

Even though a veteran may already have an existing VA loan, a new home can still be purchased without selling the old home as long as the entitlement varies substantially from the original entitlement. For example, if the original home were bought with a maximum loan guaranty of $7500, the remaining entitlement would be $28,500, which is the difference between the current guaranty of $36,000 and the maximum of $7500 at the time the original home was financed.

OCCUPANCY REQUIREMENT

The veteran must sign a Certificate of Intention to occupy the home to be purchased; this is required by the VA before the loan will be made. However, should the veteran later move to another home, the old home, financed by the VA loan, may be rented.

REPAYMENT PLANS

The VA will guarantee loans to purchase homes made with the following repayment plans:

□ *Traditional Fixed-Payment Mortgage.* This type of VA loan calls for equal monthly payments for the life or term of the loan. The maximum term is 30 years and 32 days; however, the term may never be for more than the remaining economic life of the property as determined by the appraisal.

□ *Graduated Payment Mortgage (GPM).* This repayment plan provides for smaller-than-normal monthly payments for the first few years (usually five years), which gradually increase each year and then level off after the end of the *graduation period* to larger-than-normal payments for the remaining term of the loan. The reduction in the monthly payment in the early years of the loan is accomplished by delaying a portion of the interest due on the loan each month and by adding that interest to the principal balance (referred to as *negative amortization*).

□ *Buydowns.* The builder of a new home or seller of an existing home may "buydown" the veteran's mortgage payments by making a lump-sum payment up front at closing that will be used to supplement the monthly payments for a certain period, usually three to five years.

□ *Growing Equity Mortgage (GEM)* This repayment plan provides for a gradual annual increase in the monthly payments with all of the increase applied to the principal balance. The annual increases in the monthly payment may be fixed (for example, 3 percent per year) or tied to an appropriate index. The increases to the monthly payment result in an early payoff of the loan in about 11 to 16 years for a typical 30 year mortgage.

DOWN PAYMENT REQUIREMENTS

The VA does not require a down payment by the veteran under the fixed-payment mortgage, buydown, and the GEM, up to the maximum loan amount of $144,000. However, should the veteran agree to purchase a home in excess of this limit, a 25 percent down payment is required for any amount over $144,000. In addition, a down payment is required under the GPM repayment plan because the loan balance will increase during the initial years of the loan. Therefore a down payment is necessary to keep the loan balance from exceeding the purchase price.

INTEREST RATES

The maximum interest rate on VA loans varies from time to time, based on changes in the overall mortgage market. Generally speaking, the VA mortgage interest rate is usually about 1 percent below conventional fixed-rate mortgages. Once a VA loan is made, the interest rate set in the note will remain the same for the term of the loan.

However, if the VA interest rate goes down and you still own and occupy the property securing a previous VA loan, you may apply for a new VA loan to refinance the previous loan at a lower interest rate without using any additional entitlement.

CLOSING COSTS

No commission or brokerage fees may be charged for obtaining a VA loan. However, you may pay reasonable closing costs to the lender in connection with a VA-guaranteed loan.

The closing costs generally include VA appraisal, credit report, survey, title report, recording fees, a 1 percent loan origination fee, and a VA funding fee. The closing costs and origination charge may not be included in the loan, except in VA refinancing loans.

A VA funding fee of 1 percent of the loan amount is payable at the time of closing. This fee may be included in the loan and paid from the loan proceeds. The funding fee does not have to be paid by veterans who receive VA compensation for service-connected disabilities or who but for receipt of retirement pay would be entitled to compensation or surviving spouses of veterans who died in service or from a service-connected disability.

DISCOUNT POINTS

Generally veterans are not permitted to pay discount points in connection with VA financing; these charges are usually paid by persons selling homes to VA buyers.

Lenders require discount points when they consider the maximum VA interest rate to be too low to produce the yield or income that other conventional loans would provide. Thus, points are charged to make the VA loan interest rate comparable in yield to conventional loan interest rates. The amount of points to be paid is a matter of negotiation between the seller and the lender. The VA has no direct control over the charging of discount points.

As a veteran-borrower, you may pay discount points only in connection with the following types of VA loans:

- When refinancing an existing home loan on property you own and occupy.
- When repairing, altering, or improving your home.
- When building a home on land you already own or will buy from someone other than your builder.

- In some cases, when purchasing a home from a seller that the VA determines is legally precluded from paying such a discount.

IMPOUNDS

The VA requires lenders to collect funds from the borrower to cover real estate taxes and hazard insurance premiums that are set aside in a reserve account referred to as *impounds*. This amount is prorated monthly and paid as part of the monthly mortgage payment.

VA MANUFACTURED-HOME FINANCING

The VA is authorized to guarantee loans made by private lenders to eligible veterans for the purchase of new or used manufactured (mobile) homes with or without a lot. The guaranty on a mobile home loan is an amount equal to the veteran's available entitlement, not to exceed the maximum of $20,000 or 50 percent of the purchase price, whichever is less. Therefore, $80,000 ($20,000 × 4) is the current maximum loan amount available with a 5 percent down payment. A veteran who already owns a mobile home may obtain a VA-guaranteed loan to purchase a lot on which to place the mobile home. Veterans who receive a guaranteed mobile-home loan can use their full entitlement to buy a standard home if their mobile-home loan is paid off in full.

VA interest rates for mobile-home loans vary (they're usually higher) from those established for standard home loans.

Maximum loan repayment terms are as follows: 20 years and 32 days for a single-wide unit or a combination single-wide unit and lot; 23 years and 32 days for a double-wide unit only; 25 years and 32 days for a double-wide unit and lot; and 15 years and 32 days for a lot on which to place a mobile home you already own.

Requirements for Mobile Homes

A mobile home must be built on a permanent frame and made to be moved in one or more sections. It must be built to be lived in year round by a single family and there must be permanent eating, cooking, sleeping, and sanitary facilities. A single-wide mobile home must be at least 10 feet wide, with a minimum floor area of 400 square feet; double-wide units must be at least 20 feet wide, with at least 700 square feet of floor space.

A modular home is not the same as a manufactured home for VA purposes. Although the sections of a modular home are built in a factory and then moved to a building site, the home must still be put up and completed at the building site. You may obtain a loan to purchase a modular home under the VA's regular home loan program.

A FINAL IMPORTANT NOTE ABOUT VA LOANS

Because of abuse by investors, new legislation has changed some of the features of the VA loan. As of March 1, 1988 the holder of a VA loan is now obligated to notify the VA when it has knowledge that the property has been transferred and is liable to the VA for any damages resulting from non-notification. Therefore, the lender can now charge the assumptor of a VA loan for a determination of credit worthiness.

In addition, there is a new 0.5 percent assumption fee paid by the assumptor of a VA loan.

Finally, on VA refinancings issued after January 20, 1988, the entitled veteran or spouse must occupy or must certify that he or she previously occupied the home. The amount of a refinanced loan is limited to 90 percent of the home's appraised value. The term can exceed by up to 10 years the remaining term of the loan being refinanced.

13 REFINANCING

Some homeowners encumbered with a high-interest-rate mortgage loan are likely candidates to replace, or renew, a costly mortgage with another, lower-rate mortgage. The roller-coaster interest rate ride can present great opportunity for those trapped with high loan payments on loans originated when market rates were excessive. For whatever reason, these homeowners can save substantially (under certain conditions) when they refinance during times of low market rates.

Before you go ahead and bail out that old loan, especially if the old loan has a valued low rate of interest, it would be wise to consider some of the implications of refinancing.

REASONS FOR REFINANCING

Some homeowners might want to break away (when the time is right) from certain underlying loan conditions which are unfavorable, such as:

- The existing first mortgage has an interest rate significantly higher than the current market rate.
- There is an unfavorable second mortgage with a balloon that will soon mature and the homeowner is unable to pay it.
- There is an adjustable-rate mortgage and the borrower wishes to elude the uncertainty of future rate increases.

Besides these unfavorable conditions, there are also other reasons you might want to refinance. Trading up to a bigger home while market rates are low is one possibility. Although, technically speaking, trading up is not considered refinancing, nevertheless you are ridding yourself of a high rate loan and replacing it with a cheaper one. You may want to tap the equity in your home to give you ready cash for certain things, such as a college education, new furniture, a vacation, or more real estate investments. Whatever the reason, there are considerations that have to be made, in particular the cost of refinancing.

COST TO REFINANCE

Before you consider the cost involved with refinancing, remember that refinancing an old loan with a new lender is essentially the same as originating a loan for a home purchase. The new lender will require proper applications, credit reports, and so on similar to the usual procedures for qualifying for a home purchase. You can avoid some of the hassles by keeping the replacement loan with the same lender as you had under the existing loan. This way you can save on a very important item: the prepayment penalty. Most conventional loans have a prepayment clause that allows them to charge a penalty of six months' interest for premature loan payoff. If you stay with the same lender, it is likely the prepayment penalty will be deferred, because the lender can earn points on a refinance.

You also have to consider the cost of points to refinance, usually 2 to 3 percent of the loan amount. Then you have the cost of the appraisal, credit report, and title insurance. On the average, figure about 4 points of the loan amount as a total cost to refinance. You can pay for the cost of refinancing either at time of loan issuance or it can be financed into the loan proceeds.

TAX IMPLICATIONS

Besides the cost considerations, you also should consider the tax implications of refinancing. The interest you pay on a mortgage is tax deductible. In the early years of a long-term amortized loan, the amount of interest paid is greatest and thus the deductions are also greatest. Therefore, you will lose significant tax breaks if you refinance a high-rate, long-term mortgage with a lower rate, shorter-term mortgage. In other words, if you reduce your monthly payments with a lower interest rate loan, be prepared to lose tax write-offs you had with the higher interest rate loan.

BEWARE OF RATE FLUCTUATIONS

The borrower should be alert to the rate of interest that is being applied for. Remember, market interest rates for mortgage loans are constantly changing. It should be determined whether the rate on the day of application will remain the same until the day the loan is issued. Some lenders charge the borrower a fee of up to 1 point of the loan amount to guarantee a quoted rate.

Of course, you don't have to pay this fee to establish a locked-in rate at closing. You could take an educated gamble that market rates will go down after loan application. As mentioned earlier, market interest rates follow a directional trend that sometimes can last years. They can have a rising or declining trend; seldom do they remain constant. Once the trend changes, the new direction of the trend usually develops over a period of time and endures until a new trend occurs. If you determine that the market rate for mortgage loans is declining, then it would be wise to take an educated chance that rates are unlikely to rise (or, even better, will fall) between the time of application and the loan issuance.

REFINANCING IS NOT FOR EVERYONE

Before refinancing can be beneficial, you must maintain the replacement loan for at least three years because it takes this long for lower monthly payments to make up for the total cost of refinancing. In fact, studies have shown that two basic rules of thumb are relevant to this matter.

Refinancing Rules

Rule one states that you must continue to own the refinanced home at least three years or more to enjoy the reduced monthly payment benefits. Rule two says that the rate of interest must be 2 points or more below that which you're already paying.

An example of rule two would be when the going market rate is 11 percent and the existing fixed rate on your mortgage is 14 percent. Since your rate is 14 and you could refinance at 11 (a difference of 3 points, which is more than the recommended 2 points), it would benefit you financially to refinance. If, on the other hand, the going market rate is 11 percent but your rate is 12 percent, it would not be practical (costwise) to refinance because the differential is only 1 point.

Briefly then, rules one and two combined mean that the savings in monthly payments of the new loan should, over three years, at least equal the cost to acquire it.

An alternative, if it's not good judgment to refinance because the rate on your existing loan is low and doesn't meet the requirements of rule number two, is to take out a second mortgage. A second mortgage can be arranged in many forms and is a very important tool in maintaining the value of your present low interest loan. A second mortgage could be in the form of a home improvement loan or a home equity loan. (See Chapter 14, Alternative Methods of Financing, for more information on take-out loans.)

Also, there are equity implications that should be considered, some of which are advantageous to your financial well-being. Not only do you save money by refinancing high rate loans with a lower rate, you also build up equity in your home faster. (Equity always builds faster on amortized loans with lower interest rates and on loans with shorter terms.)

Bear in mind that the equity in your home is a valuable asset. If you borrow against that equity and spend the proceeds of the loan on frivolous things, your overall net worth will decline. On the other hand, if you use the proceeds in a more prudent manner (sound real estate investments or substantial home improvements), the value of your net worth won't be eroded.

SOURCES

Your best sources for refinancing are the government-backed programs of the VA and FHA. Both these loan programs offer lower rates of interest and smaller loan origination costs than do conventional loans. Furthermore, if you decide to sell your house after you've acquired either a VA or an FHA mortgage loan, it will be more saleable because of the assumable nature of these loans. (See Chapters 11 and 12 on FHA and VA financing for more details.)

14 ALTERNATIVE METHODS OF FINANCING

In addition to government-backed programs of the VA and FHA or conventional financing, the potential homebuyer has several other methods available to finance a purchase. Under certain circumstances, the seller of the property may also be the lender, as when the property is sold under a purchase-money mortgage or land contract. The following material covers these innovative methods of financing and other alternative methods.

PURCHASE-MONEY SECOND MORTGAGE

This is a method of financing in which the seller of the property takes back a loan for the equity in the property instead of taking cash. Suppose, for example, you buy a house for $80,000 with a $5000 down payment and you assume an existing $50,000 loan. The $25,000 balance remaining is carried back by the seller in the form of a purchase-money second mortgage payable under terms you negotiate with the seller. In this example, $30,000 represents the seller's equity in the property. You pay $5000 down; instead of $25,000 cash, the seller takes back a purchase-money second mortgage of $25,000.

Terms on the $25,000 purchase-money second are negotiable and can take shape according to the needs of both the buyer and seller. For instance, probably most advantageous for the buyer would be an interest-only note for a term of 10 years. Typically, purchase-money seconds have an interest rate of 10 percent; however, this rate is negotiable. Of course, the lower the rate of interest you can negotiate for yourself, the better off you will be. I have seen second mortgages retained by sellers at interest rates as low as 8 percent and as high as 12 percent. (Certain states have usury laws which legally prevent exces-

Example of Purchase-Money Second Mortgage

Price		$80,000
Assume existing first	$50,000	
Down payment	5,000	
New purchase-money second	25,000	
Total	$80,000	

sive rates from being charged. You should find out whether the state where you reside has these limitations.)

If you do negotiate for an interest-only condition, keep in mind that nothing will be applied toward the principal balance owing and the entire principal balance will be due and payable at the end of the term. Although this is definitely a disadvantage, inflation provides the advantage of paying back the entire principal balance of the note at an extended future date with cheaper deflated dollars.

Although intertest-only is the least expensive form of note, a fully amortized note payable in monthly installments would pay off the entire amount by the end of the loan's term. This would inhibit your monthly cash flow (assuming it's income property) because of the higher monthly payment; however, the loan would be completely paid off at term's end.

There is a midrange area of negotiation between an interest-only note and a fully amortized note. You could negotiate for a partly amortized note wherein a portion of the principal amount would be paid off monthly; thus you would owe substantially less at the end of the term. Also, you could have a $25,000 balance amortzied over 20 years and payable in 10 years. This method would keep monthly payments relatively low and would help to pay off a large portion of principal during the 10 years, with only a small balance owing.

Purchase-money seconds are an integral part of profitable real estate investing primarily because you can create inexpensive seller financing that, in most cases, can be assumed by the next buyer. You can actually earn more money by keeping your interest rates low and then reselling your properties at higher rates of interest.

As an example, three years ago I found a great property that, at first glance, appeared impossible to purchase with a small down payment nor was it likely that the seller would carry back any financing. This beautiful property had an existing 8 percent first loan of $40,000, and the seller wanted $25,000 down. The list price was $119,000, and the listing agent doubted that the seller would be willing to carry back a second loan. Not to be denied, I made an offer of $92,000; I would pay

$10,000 down and assume the existing first loan of $40,000, and the seller was to carry back a second loan at 9 percent for the balance owing of $42,000. Neither my agent not the seller's agent believed this offer had a one-in-a-hundred chance of being accepted. But to everyone's surprise the seller made a counteroffer at a price of $96,000 while accepting all the financing terms of my original offer. Therefore, the only change from my original offer was the price, from $92,000 to $96,000, which increased the amount of the second loan carried back from $42,000 to $46,000. I gladly accepted the counteroffer.

Here's an illustration of that transaction:

Purchase price		$96,000
Assumed existing first loan	$40,000	
Down payment	10,000	
New purchase-money second	46,000	
Total	$96,000	

In this example, I created $46,000 in new low-interest financing on a property that, at first glance, you'd have thought would never sell under such advantageous terms. Six months after I purchased this lovely money-maker, I sold it for $115,000 on a wrap-around mortgage, and I would net $350 or more per month on it for the next 20 years. The reason I say "or more" is because once the underlying loans are paid off, which is in about 10 years, I continue to collect on the wrap without having to pay on the underlying loans. (See the Wrap-Around Mortgage section in Chapter 16, Creative Financing Strategies. The main reason for the property's profitability was the low interest rates that were maintained after the sale (8 percent on the first mortgage, 9 percent on the second; although I collected 11.5 percent on the total balance owing for 20 years).

Based on this experience, you never really know whether a seller will carry back a note unless you at least attempt to create low-interest secondary financing by making a legitimate offer.

TAKE-OUT SECONDS

A take-out second loan, also referred to as an equity loan, is different from a purchase-money second loan because it's created from equity in property already owned. For instance, you own a property with $50,000 equity in it. You could take out a second mortgage against that equity to make home improvements, pay for a college education, or buy additional income property. Institutional lenders usually fund this type of loan in amounts up to 80 percent of the equity in the property.

Take-out seconds are probably the most expensive method of financing real estate and substantially reduce your equity in the encumbered property. However, under certain conditions, take-out seconds can be favorable; for example:

- A take-out may be better than refinancing, especially if the existing first loan has a below market rate of interest.
- There is a tax loophole for equity loans. The Tax Reform Act of 1986 created a loophole that is associated with equity loans. Under the new tax law, the consumer-interest deduction is being phased out, but certain equity loans are tax deductible. In other words, because of the new tax law, it might be reasonable to take out an equity loan just to pay off all existing consumer debt, which is not tax deductible, with a new equity debt, which is tax deductible.

Keep in mind that new tax rates save no more than 15 cents on the dollar for some people and a maximum of 28 cents on the dollar for others.

A Special Note about Second, Third, Fourth, Etc., Mortgages

While we are discussing second mortgages. it is important to clear up certain misunderstandings about the safety of these loans. In the 1930s, the era of the Great Depression, many junior lien holders (second, third, etc., mortgage holders) were wiped out in a foreclosure when the borrower did not make loan payment. In those days when a first mortgage lender began foreclosure proceedings, the secondary or junior lien holders had to pay off the entire first mortgage balance to protect their second mortgage interest and to stop the foreclosure proceedings, otherwise the second mortgage interest would be wiped out in the foreclosure sale.

This is not the case today. Now if the borrower defaults on either a first or second (or third, fourth, etc.) mortgage, only the missed payments and late fees, if any, are required to be paid by the secondary lender to protect the mortgage interest. Therefore, in the event of a pending foreclosure by a prior mortgage holder, no longer is the entire balance due in one sum to protect a secondary mortgage.

SHOULD YOU REFINANCE OR TAKE OUT A SECOND?

Several important factors, such as increased property values, equity build-up, and inflation, present many property owners with the opportunity to use the accumulated equity in their home. How this money is obtained should be carefully considered by the borrower because the savings that can be earned are substantial, depending on the type of financing chosen.

Essentially, you have two choices: Either refinance your existing loan or take out a second mortgage and leave intact the existing first mortgage in order to make use of the equity in the home. Consider the following comparison of the two methods.

The decision either to refinance or to take out a second loan confronts many homeowners who have owned their home several years and would like to spend some of that accumulated equity. In most cases, the existing mortgage loan is at an interest rate below the current prevailing rate for new mortgages. If this is the case, it would be unwise to refinance because you would be eliminating the value of the existing low-interest loan by replacing it with a costlier, high-interest rate loan. However, it would be wise to refinance if the prevailing mortgage loan rate is 2 points or more below the rate that you are already paying on the first mortgage. Usually, a savings of 2 points or more is required to overcome all the costs of initiating a new loan.

Instead of refinancing, you also have the option of taking out a second mortgage loan in order to maintain the value of the present low rate of interest on the existing first loan. Let us use, for example, a home purcahsed six years ago for $50,000 with a first mortgage attached at 8 percent for a term of 30 years. Payment for principal and interest is $300 a month, and the remaining loan balance after six years of ownership is approximately $38,000. Since the current market value of the house is $80,000, you therefore have about $42,000 equity in the home.

If you refinance the house at an 11.5 percent rate of interest, the lender would advance 80 percent of the market value, of which $38,000 must be applied toward paying off the first mortgage loan. Consequently, there would be $26,000 in net proceeds ($80,000 × 80% = $64,000 − $38,000 = $26,000). The new first loan would require monthly payments of $634 to amortize principal and interest over the 30-year term.

On the other hand, if you arranged a second mortgage for an amount of net proceeds equal to that of refinancing, which is $26,000, in today's market the lender would charge you 13.5 percent. The term of

Table 14.1 Comparing Refinancing with a Take-Out Second

Refinancing			
Net Proceeds	Payment on First Loan	Term of Loan	Total Amount Paid Over Term of Loan
$26,000	$634	30 yrs	$228,240

A Take-Out Second					
Net Proceeds	Payment on First	Term Remaining on First	Payment on Second	Term Remaining on Second	Total Amount Paid Over Term of Loan
$26,000	$300	25 yrs	$338	15 yrs	$150,840

the new second loan would be 15 years with a monthly payment of $338. The total monthly payments of both first and second loans for the next 15 years would be $638 ($338 + $300). After 15 years the second loan would be paid in full; then, only a monthly payment of $300 on the existing first mortgage would be required. (See Table 14.1.)

As Table 14.1 shows, the difference paid over the entire term of the loan is a substantial savings of $77,400 when taking out a second mortgage instead of refinancing. In this particular situation, the property was refinanced at 3.5 points above the rate of the existing loan, and $38,000 went to pay off the original amount owing. This is the primary reason that refinancing costs so much more than the take-out second. In addition, although the new take-out second loan interest rate appears high at 13.5 percent, the term is short at 15 years, meaning a substantial savings in the amount of interest because of the short term of the loan.

LAND CONTRACT

Another alternative, sometimes referred to as an installment contract or contract of sale, is strictly an agreement between buyer and seller. The important thing to remember about a land contract is that the deed to the property remains with the seller until the conditions of the contract are fulfilled. The buyer retains possession of the property. However, should the buyer default on the agreement (not pay as agreed), the property reverts to the seller.

Real estate contracts can be infinitely flexible because there is no financial intermediary to put restrictive conditions into the financing. Thus, a contract is an agreement between the buyer and seller only and can be structured any way that is agreeable to both. Once the contract is signed, it is binding between the two parties.

Much like a wrap-around mortgage, land contracts are useful in wrapping existing low-interest-rate financing. And, similar to a wrap, in order to avoid complications, it's necessary for the underlying loans to be assumable.

Please note that land contracts can be riskier than mortgages and deeds of trusts. The law regarding these instruments is precise and has been well developed over the years. On the other hand, the law regarding land contracts tends to be vague and more open to judicial interpretation.

Most of the legal risk associated with land contracts is inherent with passing the deed. Under such a contract, the deed is retained by the seller until conditions of the contract are fulfilled. But what happens if the seller, for some reason, cannot deliver clear title? Tax problems, divorce, or death in the family can all create problems that might undermine the seller's otherwise well-intentioned plans.

Another potential difficulty could arise if any of the underlying loans have a due-on-sale clause. Should such an alienation clause in fact exist, the lender holding the mortgage could invoke a right to ask for the loan to be paid in full.

Some of these difficulties can be overcome if certain precautionary steps are taken. The first would be for the seller to place the deed in safekeeping with a neutral third party, such as a trustee or title company. Another would be for a similar neutral third party to receive the buyer's payment, to make payments on all the underlying obligations, and then to pay the seller what's left over from the buyer's payment.

As you can see, real estate contracts involve somewhat more risk than standard forms of financing. This, of course, does not mean contracts should not be used. Many situations, especially when low-interest, assumable financing prevails, can present opportunities for both buyer and seller under a land contract. However, it is advisable that you consult with a trusted attorney familiar with real estate contracts before involving yourself with this form of financing.

THE SHARED APPRECIATION MORTGAGE (SAM)

The SAM at a Glance

- The rate of interest is substantially lower than conventional fixed-rate mortgages.
- The borrower shares a portion of the home's increased value when the term of the loan expires or when the property is sold.
- Both the interest rate and monthly payments are fixed over the term of the loan, which is 10 years.
- The SAM is not assumable.

The shared appreciation mortgage (SAM), often referred to as the shared equity mortgage or equity participation mortgage (not the same as "equity sharing") recently evolved as a financing technique to make home ownership more accessible. The borrower receives a lower cost in financing a home in return for agreeing to share part of an increase in value with the lender.

Terms of a typical SAM would offer the borrower a discount of one-third off the prevailing market interest rate for a fixed-rate mortgage loan. In return, the lender gets one-third of any appreciation in the home at the loan term's expiration or when the property is sold.

As an example, suppose the going rate on a fixed-rate mortgage is 12 percent and you need a $70,000 loan to purchase an $80,000 home. Monthly principal and interest payments would be $720 at 12 percent. The lender could offer you a SAM at 8 percent (one-third off) which results in a monthly payment of $514. The savings is $206 per month, or $2472 annually.

Six years later, your $80,000 home is sold at a price of $125,000. One-third of the gain ($15,000) will have to be paid to the lender. If you didn't sell after six years and waited 10 years to the end of the SAM's loan term, you would have to get the home appraised, pay the lender his fair share, then refinance the expired mortgage.

The SAM presents a number of unanswered questions for the borrower. First, if the homeowner makes improvements to the home, does the lender help pay the costs? And, if he doesn't, will the lender share in the appreciation of the improvement? These questions, along with the lender's sharing in the appreciation of the home, can be avoided by the wise borrower who entirely avoids this type of financing. Life is already too complicated to involve yourself with sharing your hard-earned profits with lenders, especially with having them share in your improvements without paying the freight.

REVERSE ANNUITY MORTGAGE (RAM)

This type of loan is opposite in function to other types of loans. Typically, a homeowner receives a lump sum from the lender, then makes payment to the lender until the loan balance is paid off. Under the terms of the RAM, the homeowner does not receive a lump sum, but instead receives a monthly payment (annuity) from the lender which is applied against the equity in the home.

The reverse annuity mortgage emerged to assist elderly persons on a fixed income who have a substantial equity or who own their home free and clear. Instead of selling the home to make use of the equity, the owners can take out a RAM wherein the lender makes monthly payments to the owner in the form of an annuity. Payoff of the annuity occurs at a future date by sale of the property.

EQUITY SHARING

Another method available to finance your purchase is equity sharing, also known as shared equity, equity participation, equity partnership, and shared appreciation. This concept originated out of the need to pair cash-short buyers with cash-rich investors. These two share ownership of the property and both gain later when the property is sold for a profit.

Here's how it works. Let's say you are short of cash to make a down payment on a house and your parents want to help. Your parents agree to make the down payment in exchange for a one-half interest in the house. You agree to occupy the house, maintain it, and pay fair-market rent to your parents for their interest in the property. You and your parents split the costs of principal and interest, property taxes, and insurance. Your half-owner parents, because they are rental property owners, can claim income-tax deductions of mortgage interest, property taxes, and depreciation. (If, on the other hand, the parents had made the down payment in the form of a gift, they would receive no tax or appreciation benefits.) Your tax deductions will be the same as for all homeowners, that of mortgage interest and property taxes.

Taking title to a property under equity sharing is the same as purchasing a home on your own. Both parties go on the title according to local statutes, and both parties sign the mortgage note and take responsibility for its payment.

Equity-sharing transactions require one additional step to home ownership. A written agreement between co-owners is necessary to spell out exactly the important points of the agreement, such as ownership percentages, rent to be charged, buy-out options, specifics on resale, and responsibility for repairs and maintenance. In addition, the agreement should specify procedures in the event of death, default, disability, bankruptcy of a co-owner, or acts of God, such as floods, earthquakes, and tornadoes.

Equity sharing then can be beneficial to both the investor and the owner-occupant. The owner-occupant can eventually buy out the investor, sell the house, and use the proceeds for a down payment on another house. The investor has tax advantages from the ownership interest of a rental property and can share in the appreciation.

SPECIAL TYPES OF LOANS

There are other types of special financing, such as chattel loans and personal loans, as well as interim financing and developmental financing.

Chattel Loans

This type of loan is made on the basis of personal property rather than real property as security for the loan. Automobiles, business equipment, and pleasure boats normally qualify for security against a chattel loan.

Traditionally, these types of loans are funded for a short term and the cost is substantially higher than for home mortgage loans. This is primarily because the security for the loan is movable, as opposed to real property which is not.

Personal Loans

These loans are made on the basis of your credit worthiness without security. If you have good credit, you can usually borrow from $5000 up to $20,000 and your signature is all that's required.

Interim or Construction Financing

Construction loans are made on a short-term basis, usually two years or less, and are used to fund the construction of a new building. Security for the loan is in the underlying land plus the value of the improvement under construction.

Periodic installments of the construction loan proceeds are paid directly to the contractor or the material suppliers. Once the building is completed, permanent financing is then arranged to pay off the existing construction loan. Because of risks such as cost overruns, mechanic liens, and strikes, construction financing usually costs 2 to 3 points more in interest than permanent financing.

Development Financing

This type of funding is common when residential home builders buy a large tract of land, then build homes in phases, selling off each phase of construction as it is completed. A mortgage is used to finance the entire tract and the lender releases individual parcels from the loan as they are sold off.

Similar to construction financing, development financing is also expensive because of the additional risk borne by the lender.

15 SHOPPING FOR A NEW MORTGAGE LOAN

By this point you should have a good idea of how much house you can afford. You should also be aware that originating a new loan requires certain closing costs and a substantial down payment. Of course, how much of a down payment and how much you pay in closing costs depends on the type of loan. As a brief review, if you're entitled to a VA loan, remember it's the most favorable as you can borrow up to $144,000 with no money down at below market interest rates. The FHA loan is your second choice because only about a 5 percent down payment is required, and you can borrow up to $101,250, also at below market interest rates. Your third choice is a conventional loan that requires 20 percent down (5 percent if you pay for private mortgage insurance) at market interest rates and closing costs of 4 points or more of the loan amount.

Besides the above options, you also have to consider the type of repayment plan. This boils down to either a fixed-rate or an adjustable rate mortgage. The best alternative is the convertible ARM, which offers the best of both worlds: the lower initial rate of the ARM plus the option of conversion to a fixed rate at some future time.

If the convertible ARM is not available, then you have to decide between the standard ARM or the fixed rate mortgage. That decision, if you recall, is primarily based on the length of time you expect to maintain the loan. For four years or less the ARM is more favorable. For more than four years, the fixed-rate mortgage is probably more favorable than the adjustable rate.

WHERE TO START

Now that we have narrowed down exactly what you're looking for, it's time to start thinking about where to start looking for a new loan.

If you're already a customer of a savings and loan association (S&L) start with them. However, do not accept the first loan offered. Make a few calls to other S&Ls and compare all the costs. In addition, call mortgage bankers and realtors who may have insight into who is offering the best deals. Remember, a savings of half a percent in interest can mean a savings of thousands of dollars over the life of a long-term estate loan.

When you inquire about mortgage loans, compare more than just interest rates. Ask about the other charges you will have to pay. These include points, loan origination fee, application fee, appraisal and credit report cost, and, if applicable, the conversion fee. Also, beware of rate fluctuations. How long will the rate you're applying for be locked in? Most lenders will charge 1 point to lock in their quoted rate.

QUESTIONS ASKED OF YOU

The mortgage lender you select is primarily interested in two things: do you have the down payment and can you afford the monthly payments.

Aside from these primary queries, your lender will also ask other pertinent questions about your income, debts, bank balance, marital status, and number of dependents. The following questions are commonly asked on loan application forms:

- Are there any outstanding judgments against you?
- Have you ever been foreclosed on or given a deed in lieu of foreclosure?
- Have you ever been bankrupt?
- Are you borrowing any part of the down payment?
- Are you obligated to pay alimony or child support?
- Are you a comaker or endorser on a note?

QUESTIONS YOU SHOULD ASK

Acquiring a home loan will likely be the costliest thing you ever apply for. You will be contracting for terms that you will have to live with over a substantial period of time, until the obligation is repaid.

Thus, it is very important that you become fully informed of exactly what it is you're committing yourself to. You should use the following important questions as a guide when comparing mortgage loans and lenders:

- Is there a prepayment penalty? If so, how much?
- Is there an impound account to cover taxes and insurance?
- Is the loan assumable? If so, does the lender have the right to raise the interest rate upon assumption?
- If private mortgage insurance is required, when can I stop paying for it?
- If an ARM, when and how much are the rate adjustments?
- If a convertible ARM, how much is the conversion fee and when can I convert to a fixed rate?

SPEEDING LOAN APPROVAL

To say the least, the process of applying for a mortgage loan is a huge paper shuffle, especially under government-backed programs of the VA and FHA. The most efficient way to reduce the tedium and speed up the process is to be prepared. You can assist in the procedures by carefully collecting all the pertinent information, then making sure your loan officer gets it quickly.

Before you start, if you have any doubts about your credit, it would be advisable to get a copy of your credit report from a local agency. TRW is a national credit reporting bureau that will supply you with what you need for a small fee. This will alert you to any surprises or discrepancies listed on the report. Please note that any "negs" (negative information) that appear on your credit report will require an explanation to your lender.

In addition, here's some advice and a list of documents and financial information you'll need.

Bring your checkbook if you're applying for a conventional loan. Most lenders will charge about $300 to begin the process. This will cover the cost of the appraisal and credit report.

If you're self-employed, you'll need copies of federal income tax returns for the past two years. If not, you will have to sign employment verification forms that will be sent to your employer. You can speed up the process by informing the person with your company who is responsible for verification that the inquiry is coming and by having it sent to that particular person.

You'll need all the appropriate account numbers for bank accounts, credit cards, outstanding loans, and previous paid-off loans. Also, you'll need to submit the address and branch name of the financial institutions with whom you do business.

In conclusion, you can actually speed up the loan approval process by being prepared and supplying your loan officer with everything that is needed.

16 CREATIVE FINANCING STRATEGIES

How much you make with your real estate depends on your objectives as an investor—and on your ability to be imaginative with your resources. For some people a passive interest in a limited partnership or one piece of land is enough. But many others prefer to use real estate actively, not only to expand their holdings, but also to avoid or defer taxes.

This chapter provides the more active investor with several techniques used to finance real estate creatively.

PYRAMIDS

To *pyramid* in the investment context is to build and expand your net worth progressively from initial equity holdings. This is accomplished several ways, but essentially it is the process of borrowing against your equity in property A to buy property B. Then, as property B gains more value through inflation, you can eventually borrow against increased equity in B to purchase an additional property C.

The pyramiding technique is the oldest and fastest avenue to wealth in real estate; and rightly so, because real estate is not only a secure investment (lenders prefer it), but it can be highly leveraged. It's this high leveragibility that makes pyramiding so effective when investing in real estate.

Here's how it works. Put yourself in the position of having bought a house several years ago. You paid $60,000 for it, and now, thanks to inflation, it's worth $100,000. You obligated yourself to a $50,000 mortgage that is now down to $46,000. You could sell the house outright and gain a $40,000 profit, but then you would be subject to a tax on the gain and, more important, you would have to decide where to reinvest the proceeds from the gain. Instead, you can make use of the inflated equity in the house to begin building a pyramid.

If you decide to pyramid, you must decide on one of two alternatives to turn that equity into cash: You will either have to refinance or take out a second mortgage against your house.

How much you can get depends a lot on what local lenders will lend. This is the loan-to-value ratio, or LTVR. If the LTVR is 80 percent (average), the amount you can borrow is the value of your house times 80 percent, minus your first mortgage.

From the above example, $80,000 less a first loan of $46,000 results in $34,000 you could take from the property. Note that most lenders like to see at least 20 percent equity remaining in a property after issuing a loan.

Now that you know how much you can get, it's time to decide how you will get it. Should you take out a second loan, thus leaving intact your first mortgage, or refinance and receive an entirely new first mortgage loan?

As a rule, if you can save 2 points or more on refinancing your existing loan, it is wise to do so. But before you decide, you first must consider a few items. Does your existing mortgage have a prepayment penalty clause? If it does, then the lender will charge you a one-half of 1 percent of the loan balance as a penalty for premature payoff of the loan. (Note that VA and FHA loans do not have prepayment penalty clauses written into their mortgages.)

The prepayment penalty is only one cost you have to be aware of. There is also the costs of originating another loan. Anytime a new loan is originated the borrower will be charged, on average, about 4 percent of the loan proceeds for origination costs, which include loan origination fees, appraisal, credit report, and title search.

So, considering all these costs, you need to shave about 2 points or more from your existing mortgage interest rate for it to be economically feasible to refinance. (See a more detailed analysis of this under Take-Out Seconds in Chapter 14.)

Other than refinancing, you also have the option of taking out a second loan against your property. This approach keeps your existing low-interest-rate mortgage intact. As a rule, if your existing fixed-rate mortgage interest rate is 9 percent or less (considered low), it is better to keep this valuable asset and take out a second loan. However, if you can save 2 points or more when refinancing (eliminating a costly 14 percent loan with a new 10 percent loan), then by all means refinance. (Note: Because of the unpredictability of the adjustable-rate mortgage, only fixed-rate mortgages are used in establishing these rules about whether to refinance or to take out a second loan.)

WRAP-AROUND MORTGAGE

The *wrap*, also referred to as an all-inclusive trust deed (AITD), is an innovative method of financing real property. But remember, only assumable loans can be legitimately wrapped within a new, all-inclusive mortgage. And bear in mind that in order for a wrap-around loan to be profitable, the underlying loan(s) must be at a low, fixed rate of interest. This is because you intend to wrap the existing low-interest-rate loan with a new higher-rate loan and to earn your profit in the spread in interest rates.

This lucrative method of financing is ideal when you've got a large amount of equity in the property. Here's how it works. The wrap-around loan is used when the seller of real property wants to maintain the existing low-interest-rate loan, which in fact is assumable. The seller could allow the buyer to assume the existing loan, but wisely decides it would be more profitable to originate a new loan. Under a new wrap-around loan the seller continues making payment on the existing low-interest loan while the buyer makes payment to the seller at a higher rate on the new wrap.

This creative secondary form of financing literally surrounds (wraps) existing financing without disturbing the existing loan(s). To illustrate the complexities of the wrap, put yourself in the position of owning a home valued at $100,000, of which you owe $46,000 on a first mortgage. This particular note is assumable, and you've been paying on it for eight years at 8 percent, with 22 years remaining on the term. You could sell your house for $100,000 and, instead of allowing the buyer to assume your valuable low-interest-rate mortgage, you create a new wrap-around loan at 11 percent and issue it to the buyer. You continue paying on the existing 8 percent first mortgage for the remaining 22 years, while the buyer pays you 11 percent interest on the new wrap for the next 30 years. The 3 percent differential (spread) is your profit. It is similar to how a bank pays depositors 5 percent and then loans out these deposits at 10 percent, earning a 5 percent spread.

Thus, you sell your house for $100,000. You accept $10,000 cash down and take back a wrap-around mortgage for $90,000 at 11 percent interest for 30 years. From amortized loan tables, the buyer pays you monthly principal and interest payments of $857. You, in turn, con-

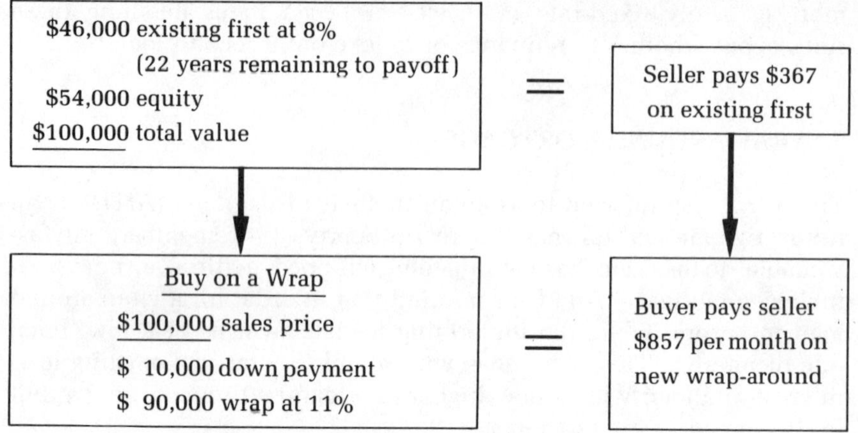

Figure 16.1. Example of a wrap-around loan

tinue paying $367 on the existing 8 percent first mortgage to give you a monthly profit of $490 for 22 years; for the remaining eight years of the wrap, you keep the entire $857 in monthly payments since the original mortgage has been paid off.

Now let's look at how much you'd lose if a wrap is not used and the buyer assumes the existing 8 percent loan. The selling price is $100,000. The buyer is to put $10,000 down and assume the existing $46,000 first mortgage at 8 percent for the remaining 22 years and the seller will carry back the remaining $44,000 at 11 percent for 30 years. The following illustrates the earnings lost by the seller when a wrap is not used to finance the property.

Payment on $46,000 assumed first loan (27 years)	$367
Payment on new $44,000 second loan at 11% (30 years)	$419
Total monthly payment is $786 for 22 years, then $419 monthly for the remaining 8 years.	
The total accumulated payments over entire terms for both loans	$247,728
Compared to a wrap-around loan at $857 monthly for 30 years	$308,520
The difference is	$60,792
which equals the earnings the seller lost by not wrapping the valuable low-interest-rate loan.	

As you can see, a wrap-around loan can be a very profitable investment. Wraps can also be very complex, especially when more than one underlying loan is involved. Try to keep the terms of your agreement simple because they can be a useful tool in either buying or selling real estate. Be sure to hire competent legal help in structuring your transaction.

ALL-INCLUSIVE TRUST DEED (AITD)

The all-inclusive trust deed is a financial instrument similar to a wrap-around mortgage, except a deed of trust is used instead of a mortgage. The buyer is the trustor on the all-inclusive note and deed of trust and the seller is the beneficiary. It is also commonly referred to as an overlapping deed of trust.

Similar to the wrap-around mortgage, the underlying loans remain intact and are "wrapped" with a new AITD. The buyer makes payment to the seller on the new AITD, while the seller in turn continues making payment on the underlying loans to the original lenders.

The AITD is most desirable when the seller wishes to benefit from low interest rates on the underlying loans. The seller can issue an AITD to the buyer with a higher rate of interest than the underlying loans, thereby benefiting from the spread in rates.

It's also advantageous when the seller is anxious to sell but is faced with a buyer who has a small down payment, or when the money market is tight and it is unlikely the buyer will qualify for a new loan.

Example of Effective Yield on an AITD

This example illustrates how yield can be increased by the seller through the use of an AITD.

For example, assume a seller wishes to sell a property for $100,000 using an AITD. The existing financing on the property consists of a first trust deed of $40,000 at 7 percent and a second trust deed of $20,000 at 8 percent, thus, the total existing loans are $60,000 and the equity position is $40,000. Should the seller issue the buyer an AITD at 10 percent and accept a $10,000 down payment, then the effective yield of seller would receive can be calculated as follows:

Seller gets 10% × $90,000 = $9000 annual interest

Seller pays on underlying loans 7% × $40,000 and 8% × $20,000 for a total of $4400.

Therefore, the seller nets $4600 interest on equity of $40,000 or an effective yield of 11.5% ($4600 divided by $40,000 = 0.115).

Advantages to the Seller

Under an AITD the seller receives a higher return as opposed to allowing the buyer to assume an existing low-interest-rate loan and carrying back a purchase-money loan for the equity. Also, the seller is likely to receive a higher price for the property under an AITD through favorable terms (the buyer is not required to pay loan origination fees).

Advantages to the Buyer

The buyer can acquire property under an AITD with a small down payment without new loan origination fees, often at an interest rate below the prevailing market rate. The AITD saves the time required to shop and apply for a new loan and the buyer is only responsible for one loan payment.

Precautionary Measures for the Buyer and Seller

(1) Seller should retain the right to approve the credit of all buyers in the event of a resale of the subject property. (2) To avoid the possibility of the property's being lost in foreclosure by failure of the seller to make payments on the underlying loans, a neutral trust such as a title company should be made responsible for receiving payments from the buyer and making existing loan payments for the seller. The cost of such an arrangement as well as who should pay for it have to be considered.

Important Points to Remember

When an AITD or wrap is used, the underlying loans cannot have a due-on-sale clause written into them or a lender may accelerate payment on them. Furthermore, the AITD or wrap-around loan is recorded as a junior lien, subject to the existing underlying loans.

"NO-MONEY-DOWN" TECHNIQUES

There are a number of methods that can be used to finance a property with nothing down. Each situation requires a different method, usually depending on the seller's requirements and whether the existing loan(s) is assumable. (Please note that closing costs are not included in the no-money-down techniques.)

Seller Requires No Cash

If the seller requires no cash and there is an assumable loan, the buyer can simply assume the existing loan and have the seller carry back a second loan for the balance of the purchase price. Obviously, this is the least complicated method of acquiring real property with no money down.

Seller Requires to Be Cashed Out

For example, you locate a house that can be purchased for $60,000 and there is an underlying $50,000 VA loan that the seller will allow to be assumed. If the seller needs to be cashed out, there are two alternatives. You could borrow the down payment of $10,000 and assume the balance owing. Or a somewhat more complicated alternative is available. Remember, in Chapter 3, when discounted notes were discussed? Well, discounting a note is part of the formula for buying with no money down when the seller has to be cashed out. Here's how it works.

The problem is, "How can the seller obtain cash for the $10,000 equity interest in the house." One method would be to convert the $10,000 note to cash. But, if you recall, to convert a note to cash usually requires a discount. Let's say an investor will buy the note at a 25 percent discount. If this is the case, the holder of the note would only receive $7500 in cash for a $10,000 note. But what if the seller requires the full $10,000 for the equity interest and won't accept the reduced amount of $7500? Then the solution is to increase the note's value to $13,333 and discount it 25 percent, which would yield the required $10,000. (The formula requires you to divide the reciprocal of the 25 percent discount, which is 75 percent, into $10,000. The result is the amount of the note required that, when discounted 25 percent, yields $10,000.)

Obviously, this solution requires the buyer to pay a premium for the property, in this case an additional $3333. However, the buyer should be reminded that paying a premium isn't all that bad as long as the buyer is not overpaying for the property. Also, because the property is purchased with no money down, maximum leverage is attained by the investor.

SIX-MONTH ROLLOVER, 100 PERCENT FINANCED

This technique is based on the theory that a cash purchase commands a bargain price and the seller is highly motivated to sell. It involves paying cash (which you borrow) for property, quickly renovating it, then reselling it at a profit. When the property is sold, the borrowed money is immediately paid back, and you earn a profit.

For example, let's say you have located a particular property that, if purchased for $67,000 cash and renovated, could be sold within six months for $100,000. For the benefit of this example we presume that you have a lender that will lend you $72,000 for six months. Table 16.1 illustrates how the numbers work.

From the example in Table 16.1, the finance cost is calculated as follows: Typically, in today's market a financial institution or private lender would fund such a loan, including renovation costs, at 14 percent interest plus 4 points. The loan proceeds consist of $72,000, of which $67,000 represents the purchase price and $5000 is the cost of renovation. Interest on $72,000 for six months is $5040, plus 4 points at a cost of $2880, for a total of $7920. Although this cost to finance may, at first glance, seem excessive, this investment technique supports such a high finance cost because of such a great net profit, especially considering this technique does not use any of your own funds.

If, by chance, you are fortunate enough to possess enough ready cash to use the six-month rollover technique without borrowing the required working capital, then obviously you are that much further ahead because you save $7920 in finance charges.

The sales commission is another variable included in the analysis. Because of the short period of time involved in this method, I usually

Table 16.1 Six-Month Rollover, 100 Percent Financed

Purchase price		$67,000
Less expenses to acquire and renovate		
Closing costs	$ 500	
Cost to renovate	5,000	
Cost to finance	7,920	
Tax and insurance (6 months)	300	
Utilities (6 months)	200	
Total expenses	$13,920	
Total expenses and purchase price		$80,920
Property is sold for $100,000		$100,000
Less selling expenses		
Sales commission (6%)	$ 6,000	
Closing costs	500	
Total expenses and purchase price	$80,920	
Total overall expense	$87,420	
Net profit before taxes		$ 12,580

find it necessary to pay a commission to procure a quick sale. However, if you can make a sale without the services of an agent, you would earn an additional $6000.

Ingredients of the Short-Term Rollover

The key to this investment technique, assuming the working capital is to be borrowed, is to have a lender tentatively arrange for such a transaction. Then, once a property you wish to invest in is located, you make an offer contingent upon acquiring sufficient financing. If your offer is accepted, it is then analyzed by your lender. Should the lender agree, then you're in business; if not, your offer would then be nullified because of the financing contingency inserted into your offer to purchase.

To profit from this innovative method, certain rules must be applied and only certain properties qualify. You can use this rule of thumb when purchasing a property: If you buy it at no more than two-thirds of its selling price after it's fixed up, you made a good deal. For instance, in our example the purchase price was $67,000, which is two-thirds the selling price of $100,000. If you purchase a home for $80,000, the selling price would have to be $120,000 to incorporate the two-thirds ratio.

Properties which best qualify are those that have a substantial amount of equity and the seller is unwilling to carry back a note; they require much renovation, yet are sound in structure and overall construction. A large amount of equity means the seller has, in most cases, owned the property for an extended period. Since it was bought for substantially less than the current selling price and the seller is unwilling to carry a note or renovate the property, the seller would be inclined to sell at a bargain price in order to be totally cashed out of the property.

Let's detail this method again just to illustrate exactly what happens. To begin with, you need a lender who will advance the entire proceeds, including renovation capital. You purchase the property using the loan proceeds to pay all the existing loans in full and to pay the seller cash for the equity. The lender then creates a new first mortgage on the subject property. With the renovation capital, you refurbish the property, then sell at a substantial profit. When the property is sold, you pay off the lender with a new first mortgage arranged by the buyer and you earn the difference, which is the profit.

BUYDOWNS

Buydowns are an interest rate subsidy paid for by the seller. Usually provided by a builder of new homes, the buydown not only saves the buyer money on a reduced interest rate, it also makes it easier to qualify for a loan.

For example, suppose a builder of a new tract of homes is faced with a soft real estate market coupled with high interest rates. A tract of new homes has just been finished and while the homes are unsold, payments still have to be made to the lender that financed the project. If buyers are not found soon, he will be in financial difficulty. Since interest rates are high, it is this builder's belief that if potential buyers could be offered an attractive financing package, the inventory of new homes could be sold. Therefore, the builder decides to use the buydown approach.

The builder contacts a local lender and together they come up with an attractive loan package. The builder will subsidize, or buydown, the interest rate to make the financing more appealing to prospective buyers. Here's how it is done.

The prevailing market interest rate is 12 percent, which means that a borrower obtaining a $70,000 loan for 30 years would have monthly payments of $720. The builder decides to offer a 9 percent interest rate, therefore shaving 3 points off the prevailing market rate. This subsidized rate will last for three years if the buyer agrees to obtain financing from the contracted lender. By borrowing $70,000 for 30 years at 9 percent, homebuyers will have payments of only $563 for those first three years. The results are that potential home buyers come to look at the homes, realize they can save $157 a month (a sum of $5652) during the buydown period, and home sales begin to flourish. The home builder/seller has to consider this $5652 subsidy cost paid on each home sold. It will be a cash payment made to the lender who underwrites these loans.

Buydowns can be a very effective marketing technique, especially in a slow real estate market when interest rates are high.

Buydown Terms

Terms of a buydown can be structured any way the seller wishes, although a typical buydown has a term of two to six years. Other popular methods of the buydown offer an extremely low interest rate initially, which gradually increases 1 point a year for five or six years. Some methods offer a very low fixed rate and others offer an attractive adjustable rate. Some builders might even offer the buyer the choice of a fixed- or adjustable-rate mortgage.

Taking Advantage of the Buydown

Now consider this interesting observation. Buydowns are generally offered on new construction of single-family homes and condominiums or on condominium conversions. The builder quite often will include the cost of the buydown directly into the overall costs. This is because many sellers—and builders in particular—know that they can get a higher price for a house if they can provide low-cost financing. If this is the case, the buyer could not only receive a buydown but, during a slow real estate market, also negotiate for a lower price.

Although buydowns are popular among new home builders, there's no reason why a buydown cannot be used by a sophisticated individual seller. To offset the cost of the buydown, the individual seller could increase the selling price of the home.

Buydown Considerations

The following are important considerations the buyer should make when utilizing a buydown.

The buyer should be aware of what happens when the term of the buydown expires. In other words, what type of financing is the buyer responsible for after the subsidy is used up? If financing by the same lender continues, what are the terms? Will it be fixed rate or adjustable rate? If it is an adjustable rate, how often will the rate be adjusted? And will there be any rate or payment caps?

The buyer should know when the buydown interest rate will change.

The buyer should know what the interest rate will become after each periodic adjustment.

Finally, the buyer must realize that the buydown does not endure the entire term of the mortgage and must prepare for when the mortgage interest rate increases and must anticipate how to handle the increased cost. The buyer must also be aware that the seller is likely to have included the cost of the buydown in the selling price. Although it is difficult to determine if, in fact, the seller has done this, none the less, the shrewd buyer who is offered a buydown should also negotiate for a price concession.

17 SOURCES OF REAL ESTATE FINANCING

It definitely pays to shop around when you need a real estate loan. If you can save just 1 point on long-term financing, you actually save thousands of dollars over the lifetime of the loan. Today, more than ever before, there is an abundance of real estate funding available for the informed investor to sclect from.

EXISTING PROPERTY SELLERS

In the home sale market the best and least expensive source of funding is the seller, especially the motivated seller. Motivated sellers are the ones who will do almost anything to stimulate the sale of their property. This includes accepting a note for the equity in their home at terms that are very advantageous for the buyer. Even without a motivated seller, one can usually acquire a second loan at rates and terms far better than one could from a conventional lender.

Here's what you save when the seller carries back a mortgage (purchase-money mortgage) and you avoid originating new financing. Originating new financing from institutional lenders typically requires the following expenditures of the borrower: credit report (an investigation into your credit history) at a cost of $100; an appraisal at $150; a loan origination fee of at least 2 percent of the loan proceeds; an interest rate at prevailing market rates; and finally, a loan that will not be assumable by another buyer.

Seller financing is obviously more convenient and requires none of these loan origination costs. In addition, you can usually negotiate a rate of interest below market rates. Furthermore, seller financing can be structured to be fully assumable, which allows you more flexibility when you sell.

SAVINGS AND LOAN ASSOCIATIONS

Savings and loans associations (S&Ls) are the primary source of new permanent financing of residential real estate. They make conventional loans as well as loans under VA and FHA programs. Typically they lend 80 percent of the value of the home and will go as high as 95 percent when the borrower is willing to pay the additional cost of private mortgage insurance. Under terms of refinancing, S&Ls tend to be more conservative and will usually lend only 80 percent of the home's value.

The chief business of S&Ls is residential real estate loans; however, they are permitted to underwrite a limited amount of construction, home improvement, and mobile home financing.

COMMERCIAL BANKS

Banks are not considered a primary source of residential real estate financing because commercial banks are not specifically organized to handle the long-term nature of real estate loans. They prefer to invest in short-term business and consumer loans that earn a higher rate of interest. They are a major source of construction financing.

Commercial banks can either be state or federally chartered. State-chartered banks must comply with the regulations of a state banking board or commission; national banks are under the jurisdiction of the Federal Reserve System. The Federal Deposit Insurance Corporation (FDIC) insures deposits of its members up to $100,000. State banks may also belong to the FDIC but must comply with state regulations.

MUTUAL SAVINGS BANKS

Their origins are similar to those of S&Ls. They operate predominantly in the northeastern sector of the United States. They are all state chartered and mutually owned by their depositors, although managed by an elected group of trustees. These institutions primarily invest their funds in long-term real estate loans, although a limited amount of their portfolio will consist of personal and consumer-type loans.

CREDIT UNIONS

Credit unions are an excellent source of take-out second mortgage loans and personal or installment vehicle loans. They usually do not provide permanent financing. Credit unions often are owned in part by their shareholders and operate on thin margins of profit, which allows them to offer more liberal terms than conventional lenders.

If you have the opportunity to belong to a credit union, by all means do so. They can be an excellent source both for short-term funding and for some intermediate-term, secured real estate loans as well.

INSURANCE COMPANIES

Insurance companies accumulate large sums of capital from the premiums paid by their policyholders. A portion of this money must be held in reserve to satisfy claims and to pay operating expenses. That which is not held in reserve is invested to attain a high yield, yet at a low risk to provide safety for the policyholder's money. The greater part of their investment portfolio is in long-term real estate loans; however, they operate differently from banks and S&Ls. They prefer to invest their money in large, long-term loans on commercial and industrial properties (office buildings and shopping centers). To improve their yield, they require equity participation (part of the profits) in order to originate the loan.

Insurance companies also invest in large packages of real estate loans that are available for resale in the secondary mortgage market.

FORMATION OF LIMITED PARTNERSHIPS

Another source of financing for real estate, especially when the investment is beyond one person's financial ability, is to form a partnership with other investors. You would be surprised how many potential investors there are who have the money but do not have the time or the ability to invest on their own. Ideal prospects are those who can better use their time working at their profession—such as doctors, dentists, and lawyers—rather than locating and renting out property.

Successful partnerships begin with the understanding that the limited partners (investors only) will be consulted only on major decisions, such as selling or refinancing the property, and that the general partner is responsible for managing the property. Investors should only invest in such partnerships when they will not need their investment capital for the specified duration of the partnership.

Before starting any partnership, you should consult with a trusted attorney to get assistance on drafting all the documents. If you plan to invest as a limited partner, look into the general partner's past experience to arrive at some indication of the potential results.

THE SECONDARY MORTGAGE MARKET

Besides the primary mortgage market, which is the interaction of the borrower with the original lender, there also exists a secondary mortgage market which gives liquidity and flexibility to the overall mortgage lending system. When a lender takes over a loan originated by another lender, he is engaging in secondary mortgage market activity.

Operatives in the secondary mortgage market buy lenders' mortgages, thus supplying them with needed cash to originate new loans. Before the emergence of the secondary mortgage market, lenders were often faced with liquidity problems. For example, suppose a long-term lender originates a 30-year mortgage loan. Although the lender will ultimately recover the principal and earn a substantial amount of interest on the transaction, assets are tied up for 30 years. These assets, which otherwise might have been available for other, possibly more lucrative investment, are in effect frozen. If all one's assets are in loans of similar durations, the lender is most definitely in an illiquid position.

Thus, the dilemma of liquidity is overcome by the buying and selling of loans in the secondary mortgage market. The principal operatives in the secondary mortgage market are the Federal National Mortgage Association (FNMA), the Government National Mortgage Association (GNMA), and the Federal Home Loan Mortgage Corporation (FHLMC).

Federal National Mortgage Association

The FNMA, referred to as "Fannie Mae," originated in 1938 for the purpose of buying and selling government-insured mortgages to assist originators of these loans in liquidating their portfolios. These acquisitions of mortgages are funded by selling notes and debentures. FNMA buys only certain mortgages of FHA/VA origination that have been funded under strict guidelines. Also the FNMA requires that all sellers purchase FNMA stock.

FNMA conducts biweekly auctions in order to buy mortgages. Before the auction the FNMA announces how much money it has available and then commits itself to making certain purchases. The FNMA bases the amount of buying and selling it does on the nation's overall economic climate. During times of tight money, when available mortgage money is in short supply, FNMA will buy. In times of loose money, the FNMA sells to investors. This so-called reverse market policy helps to stabilize the overall secondary mortgage market.

Government National Mortgage Association

Founded in 1968, the Government National Mortgage Association, referred to as "Ginnie Mae," is administrated by the Department of Housing and Urban Development. Created to take over certain programs phased out of FNMA, the GNMA is authorized to do the following: manage and liquidate part of the FNMA loan portfolio; operate federally funded housing; and oversee high-risk mortgage financing programs and the sale and purchase of government-backed securities.

The GNMA also participates with private lenders in the purchase of large blocks of loan commitments. Portions of these loan commitments are then sold as securities to the public, backed by a guarantee of the United States Treasury.

Federal Home Loan Mortgage Corporation

The Federal Home Loan Mortgage Corporation (FHLMC), referred to as "Freddie Mac," was founded in 1971. Similar to the other operatives, its purpose is to allow savings and loans to maintain liquidity for their mortgage assets. The FHLMC buys mortgages from these institutional lenders, supplying them with cash to originate new loans. Similar to the FNMA, Freddie Mac is funded by selling securities on the open market.

PRIVATE MORTGAGE INSURANCE (PMI)

Numerous private mortgage insurance companies are now insuring real estate loans in a manner similar to that of the FHA. A portion of the loan is insured against default by a premium (usually one-quarter to one-half percent of the loan proceeds) charged to the borrower.

As an example, a conservative savings and loan is likely to lend a maximum of 80 percent of a property's value; the buyer is required to put 20 percent down. However, because of the availability of PMI, the borrower could put a minimum of 5 percent down and the lender would finance the remaining 95 percent if the borrower was willing to pay the additional cost of PMI. The PMI would insure the lender against loss of the additional 15 percent invested in the property.

PMI allows lenders to make higher loan-to-value ratios, thereby allowing more buyers to purchase with less of a down payment.

LOAN BROKERS

Loan brokers, sometimes referred to as mortgage brokers, are individuals who are licensed to act as financial intermediaries between lender and borrower. They locate potential borrowers, process loan applications, and submit the applications to the lenders for final approval.

Frequently loan brokers work with or for mortgage banking companies. In some cases loan brokers are also real estate brokers who offer these lending services in addition to their normal real estate brokerage activities. (Under conflict of interest laws, some states require that one individual cannot act in both capacities in a single transaction.)

The loan brokers provide organized solutions to a variety of problems related to real estate financing today. They bring the borrower and lender together and monitor the many legal safeguards and other controls available to assure the security of the transaction. To fulfill their obligation, they must not only protect the individual lender but the borrower as well.

As mentioned, licensed real estate brokers in some states are authorized to act as loan brokers. In practice, some real estate brokers arrange loans and others sell real estate; the two tend to specialize. The loan broker arranges financing through private lenders for prospective homebuyers who do not have sufficient funds to make up the difference between a first mortgage and the total sales price. The loan broker serves the real estate salesperson as a clearing house of available loans, freeing the realtor to concentrate on sales.

Loan brokers serve the borrower by arranging funds that might otherwise not be available for specific needs. One such instance would be when a prospective home buyer does not have the difference between the first mortgage and total sales price. Another would be when a homeowner requires funds for an emergency but doesn't have adequate credit or collateral except for a home. In either event, the loan broker could arrange for secondary financing through a private lender.

MORTGAGE BANKING COMPANIES

These companies operate similarly to mortgage brokers inasmuch as they primarily act as loan correspondents. They originate real estate loans with money belonging to other institutions, such as insurance companies and pension funds or individuals, acting as an intermediary between lender and borrower.

As the originator of mortgage lending, a mortgage banker will often work with specific investors, seeking borrowers for the investors' funds and servicing the loans after origination. Loan service consists of activities such as billing, collection, making tax and insurance payments, and handling defaults if necessary. The fee for such service is usually 1 to 2 percent of the loan appropriated.

Mortgage bankers are usually organized as stock companies. As a source of real estate financing, they are subject to less stringent restrictions and limitations than S&Ls and commercial banks.

OTHER SOURCES OF FUNDS

There are essentially four other sources for mortgage loans. They are the Farmers Home Administration, the Federal Land Bank, real estate investment trusts, and trust funds.

Farmers Home Administration

A division of the Department of Agriculture, the Farmers Home Administration administers direct housing loans, insured loans, and grants to rural families. To qualify for a loan, a rural family must show its inability to obtain a loan from private sources. The rural property used for collateral is required to be within an area not to exceed a population of 10,000 (20,000 under certain circumstances).

Federal Land Bank

Established in 1916, the Federal Farm Loan Act created the Federal Land Bank. Under this act, loans can be issued for agricultural purposes to buy land and erect buildings. To join this association, each borrower is required to buy stock equivalent to 5 percent of the loan amount, which is refundable when the loan is repaid. Should the association earn money, the borrower is paid dividends on the stock. If the association loses money, it has recourse to the stock of the borrower/stockholder.

Loan-to-value ratios are a maximum of 85 percent. Therefore, the borrower could get a maximum of an $85,000 loan on property valued at $100,000. The cost to the borrower is a stock purchase of $4250 (5 percent of the loan amount).

Real Estate Investment Trusts

The real estate investment trust (REIT) was established by Congress in 1960 (effective January 1, 1961). The original purpose of the REIT was to offer the average taxpayer an opportunity for a tax-sheltered investment. Today, this is no longer the case because income from a REIT is treated as dividend income and can no longer shelter other forms of income.

A REIT is a special form of ownership in real estate that allows a widely held entity to own property and use the trust as a conduit to pass through the income to its owners without the entity incurring a tax. A group of investors pool their funds in an entity that invests in a diversified portfolio. A REIT is to real estate what a mutual fund is to stocks.

REITs offer two key advantages similar to a mutual fund: diversification and liquidity. Diversification comes from the sizable portfolio which a REIT can own. Liquidity comes from the investor's ability to sell shares of the REIT, which are usually sold on a major stock exchange. (It is fundamentally easier to liquidate shares of publicly traded stock than to dispose of individual real estate investments.)

To qualify as a REIT, the following tests must be met:

1. It must be managed by one or more trustees.
2. Ownership interests must be evidenced by transferable shares.
3. It cannot hold property primarily for sale to customers in the ordinary course of its trade or business.
4. Shares of the REIT must be held by 100 or more beneficial owners.
5. It must elect to be treated as a real estate investment trust.
6. Seventy-five percent of its assets must be invested in cash, government securities, and real estate.
7. At least 95 percent of its gross income must be derived from dividends, interest, rents on real property, or gains from the sale of real estate securities.
8. Less than 30 percent of its gross income must be from the sale of stocks and securities held for less than six months, real property

held for less than four years, and interests in mortgages on real property held less than four years.

Finally, there are three types of REITs.

1. *Equity Trusts.* This form of REIT invests only in equity interests in return for rental income, such as an apartment or office building.
2. *Mortgage Trusts.* This form of REIT only invests in real property mortgages in exchange for interest income.
3. *Combination Trusts.* This is the most popular form of REIT. It combines some equity interest and some mortgage investment.

Trust Funds

Monies placed in a trust with a trustee for the benefit of a third person or the person placing these funds is considered a trust fund. The trustee is responsible for prudently investing these funds.

Compared to financial institutions, trustees have a broader scope of investments they can make. In certain cases, they will lend money on commercial development and other projects that some institutional lenders are reluctant or prohibited by law to lend money on.

18 HOW TO FINANCE HUD-OWNED PROPERTIES

Properties owned by the Department of Housing and Urban Development (HUD) are a great source of investment for anyone. These properties have previously been foreclosed on, were financed under VA and FHA loan programs, and are now owned by HUD.

TYPES OF PROPERTIES AVAILABLE FROM HUD

- Vacant lots
- Single-family detached residences
- Duplex or two units on one lot
- Triplex (three units)
- Fourplex (a four-unit building)
- Planned unit development (PUD)
- Condominiums

SALES POLICY

HUD policy is to sell to anyone regardless of race, color, creed, or sex who can meet the down payment, credit, and certain other requirements. Not only prospective owner-occupants but investors may purchase as well.

HUD lists properties for sale on an open basis with licensed real estate brokers. Offers to purchase are submitted by brokers on behalf of prospective purchasers, and HUD pays the broker's commission at closing. Showing properties to potential buyers, preparing the HUD-9548 Standard Real Estate Contract and Addenda, and following up on all paperwork required for closing a transaction are the primary responsibilities of the selling broker. Buyers may not submit offers directly to HUD except in circumstances where they cannot obtain the services of a licensed broker.

HUD PROPERTY IS PURCHASED IN "AS-IS" CONDITION

All HUD properties are sold as is, without warranties. There will be no further alterations or additions made by the seller, and any other statements or representations made as to the condition of the property are not binding on the seller. It is the buyer's responsibility to make a determination as to the condition of the property.

FINANCING THE SALE

HUD properties are listed for sale either with or without HUD mortgage insurance. For those properties listed with HUD insurance, the buyer may seek an FHA-insured loan from a private lender and use the mortgage proceeds to buy the home from HUD. For properties listed without HUD insurance, the terms are cash in 30 days, with no contingences for financing.

As-Is Sales

This program offers properties for sale in an unrepaired or as-is condition for cash. Under this program the sale is not contingent upon the buyer's ability to obtain financing.

Property Condition. The property is unrepaired and does not meet HUD's minimum standards for mortgage insurance. In addition, it may have local code violations. HUD does not allow repairs or modifications, even at the buyer's expense, on properties listed as-is before closing.

Warranty. Buyers should be cautioned that HUD provides no warranty and that the property may have code violations.

Financing. HUD will provide financing costs for uninsured sales under the best offer addendum.

Earnest Money Deposit. Real estate brokers collect an earnest money deposit, regardless of the method of sale. The minimum is

$500 or 5 percent of the listing price, not to exceed $2000. Sales of vacant lots require 50 percent of the listing price as the earnest money deposit. Delivery of the deposit along with the sales contract and addenda are the responsibility of the selling broker.

Down Payment. Because the sale is all cash to HUD there is no down-payment requirement. However, if conventional financing is arranged, then the lender's requirements apply.

Tie Bids. A public drawing resolves bids determined to be equally advantageous to HUD.

Time Allowed for Closing the Sale. The buyer is allowed 30 days to close the sale after HUD signs the sales contract.

Insured Sales

This program offers properties that are eligible for FHA-insured mortgage financing. Such financing requires the buyer to have acceptable mortgage credit and the sale is contingent on the buyer's being approved. FHA-insured financing is not required and buyers may obtain other financing. However, if the buyer uses another form of financing, then the purchase becomes an as-is, all-cash transaction.

Property Condition. Properties which HUD selects for sale with FHA-insured financing appear to meet the intent of HUD's minimum property standards for existing dwellings, based on available repair estimates. HUD does not, however, certify that the property is without defects, and buyers should be cautioned to make their own determination of a property's condition before submitting an offer.

Warranty. Buyers should be cautioned that HUD provides no warranty whatsoever pertaining to condition of the property.

Financing. FHA-insured financing is available upon buyer qualification under various programs discussed later in this chapter.

Earnest Money Deposit. Real estate brokers are required to collect a minimum $500 deposit or 5 percent of the listing price, not to exceed $2000. Sales of vacant lots require 50 percent of the listing price as a deposit.

Down Payment. Owner-occupant buyers are required to make a down payment of 3 percent of the listing price, up to $101,250. Investors are required to put at least 15 percent down. Sample computations are provided under Calculating Down Payments, below.

Owner-Occupant Priority. In the event of a tie bid, HUD will give priority to an owner-occupant's bid over that of an investor.

Time Allowed for Closing the Sale. The buyer is responsible for making sure that credit information is received by HUD as soon as possible after acceptance of the offer. Generally, the sale should be closed within 45 days after HUD's acceptance of the offer.

Mortgage Insurance Premium. The MIP is now collected in one lump sum at the time of closing, either in cash or the mortgagor may finance it.

CALCULATING DOWN PAYMENTS

The following are examples of how to calculate down payments under the various programs:

Insured Sales to Owner-Occupants

Owner-occupants can finance 97 percent of the list price up to $101,250 and 90 percent of the bid exceeding the listing price.

Example 1

List price		$90,000
Buyer's bid	90,000	
The down payment is 3% of $90,000	2,700	
Total down payment	$ 2,700	

Example 2

List price		$85,000
Bid price	88,000	
The down payment is 3% of $85,000	2,550	
Plus 10% of bid above list price	300	
Total down payment	$ 2,850	

Insured Sales to Investors

Investors are required to make a 15 percent down payment and can finance the balance of the sales price, up to local maximums.

List price		$60,000
Bid price	62,000	
The down payment is 15% of $62,000	9,300	
Total down payment	$ 9,300	

FHA MORTGAGE INSURANCE PROGRAMS

The FHA has several programs available to finance property listed under the insured sale program. A buyer can obtain an FHA loan from an institutional lender and use the loan proceeds to buy property from HUD. FHA-insured financing is available under any of the following two repayment plans:

Section 203(b) Mortgage

This is the most common and popular 30-year, fixed-rate mortgage. Before January 1, 1987, all FHA loans were fully assumable without qualification. Under current regulations, FHA fixed-rate loans originated after this date can only be assumed after two years (one year if owner occupied) has elapsed from loan origination date.

Section 245(a): Growing Equity Mortgage (GEM)

Under this loan program, scheduled increases in monthly payments during the early years are applied directly to principal reduction. For more details regarding the GEM, see Chapter 12, VA Financing.

19 INCOME TAX IMPLICATIONS OF REAL ESTATE OWNERSHIP

Real estate ownership offers the average family bountiful tax shelter benefits that are nonexistent with other forms of investments. Recent tax reform has eliminated or reduced tax shelter benefits on most other investments. Real estate's ability to shelter income has also been slightly reduced by recent reforms, but it still remains the preferred tax shelter.

The object of this chapter is to unravel and simplify the complicated tax laws that pertain to real estate and assist you in tax planning, enabling you to work proficiently with your tax planner or attorney and save money on income taxes.

HOMEOWNER TAX SAVINGS

You can avoid or defer tax on the gain from the sale of your home depending on certain conditions and your age.

Deferring Tax on the Sale of a Residence

You can defer tax on the gain from the sale of your home if you meet the following three tests:

1. *Principal residence test.* This test requires that you have used your old house as your principal residence and you now use, or intend to use, your new house as a principal residence. Only one principal residence, for tax deferral purposes, is allowed at any one time. You cannot defer tax on the profitable sale of a principal residence by purchasing a summer cottage nor can you defer the tax on the sale of a second home.

2. *Time test.* This test requires that within two years of the sale of

your old house, you buy, or build, a new house as a principal residence.

3. *Investment test.* This test requires that you buy or build a house for an amount equal to, or more than, that received from the sale of the old house. If the replacement house costs less, part or all of the gain is taxed.

Exchanging or trading houses is considered the same as a sale for tax deferral purposes. If you make an even exchange, or pay additional cash, there is no tax on the trade. However, if you receive cash in the trade for the replacement house, you generally realize a taxable gain.

Tax-Free Residence Sale

You can avoid tax on profits up to $125,000 once in a lifetime if you are 55 or older when you sell or exchange your principal residence. In order to claim this exclusion, you must: (1) elect to avoid tax; (2) be 55 or older before the date of sale; and (3) have owned and occupied the house as your principal residence for at least three years prior to the sale. You cannot use this exclusion when you sell only a partial interest in the home.

If you and your spouse own the home jointly and file a joint return in the year of the sale, only one of you need meet the age requirement of 55 or older and qualify under ownership and residency requirements three out of the last five years.

Use caution when taking the tax-free election. Because this is a once-in-a-lifetime exclusion, consider using the tax deferral method when the gain from the sale of your home is substantially less than the $125,000 exclusion and you plan to reinvest the proceeds in a replacement home. If, for example, you did qualify for the $125,000 exclusion and, after the sale of your home, the gain was only $15,000 and you elected to exclude it, you will have used up your once-in-a-lifetime exclusion. You could defer this gain if you buy a replacement house at a cost equal to or more than the sales price of the old house. Later, when you sell the replacement house without a further home purchase, the election to exclude the gain can be made.

INTEREST DEDUCTIONS AND REFINANCING

The main tax considerations are: (1) Mortgage interest is deductible on two homes only, capped at $1 million in interest deductions annually (1988 and after). (2) Interest deductions on investments are limited to the amount of net investment income. (3) Interest deduction for a home equity loan is limited to $100,000 (1988 and after).

Deductions for interest paid on refinancing your mortgage are allowed up to the purchase price of your property plus the cost of any improvements you've made. You may not claim a deduction for interest paid on that portion of a mortgage loan that at the time the debt is incurred is greater than the cost of improvements and purchase price of the property. The tax law does make an exception to this rule: You can deduct interest on that part of a mortgage or equity loan that exceeds the purchase price and cost improvements if you use the excess loan proceeds to pay educational or medical expenses. On the other hand, if you were to take out a personal loan not secured by a residence to send your child to college, the interest on that loan is not deductible.

The rule for limiting deduction on the home's appreciated value was implemented to prevent taxpayers from borrowing against home appreciation, using the moncy to pay off consumer purchases, then deducting the interest.

Let's assume you decide to refinance your home, which is worth $100,000. You originally paid $40,000 and have made $10,000 in improvements. The lender will allow you to refinance up to $80,000, but you may write off the interest on only $50,000 ($40,000 purchase price plus $10,000 in home improvements).

If you accept the lender's maximum loan of $80,000, the interest charged by the lender on the $30,000 in excess of purchase price plus improvements is nondeductible personal interest if used for other than trade, business, or investment purposes. However, if the excess $30,000 of the loan proceeds is used to pay educational or medical expenses, all interest on the $80,000 loan is tax deductible.

What home improvements qualify to increase the amount you can borrow? A home improvement is considered generally to include all expenditures that add value to your home and last for an extended period, such as a swimming pool, new roof, new patio or deck, siding, built-in appliances, built-in cabinets, alarm system, hot water heater, new sidewalk, replacement windows, insulation, and certain landscaping.

What mortgage loans are affected by these rules? All home loans originated after August 16, 1986, are subject to the latest tax laws. Home mortgage loans that were outstanding on this date will not be affected unless they exceed the fair market value of the home at that date. Also, the mortgage interest on one additional home, such as a vacation home, qualifies for the mortgage interest deduction. See rules concerning vacation homes in this chapter.

DEDUCTING EXPENSES WHEN RENTING OUT PART OF YOUR HOME

That part of your home you occupy is handled differently for tax purposes from a rented part. Rental income and expenses allocated to the rented portion of the property are reported on Schedule E. The expenses allocated to the rental part are deductible, whether or not you itemize deductions. Deductions for interest and taxes on your personal part of the property are itemized deductions. For example, assume you purchased a fourplex in 1972 and you occupy one unit as a personal residence. You purchased it for $50,000 ($42,000 for the building and $8,000 for the land). You can depreciate 75 percent of the building cost over 27.5 years. Therefore, the cost basis for depreciation is $31,500 over 27.5 years or $1145 annual depreciation deduction. Table 19.1 shows how to deduct expenses:

Table 19.1 Deductible Expenses

	Total	Deduct Itemized Deductions	Deduct on Rent Schedule	Not Deductible
Interest	$1600	$400	$1200	
Taxes	800	200	600	
Repairs	100		75	25
Depreciation	1145		1145	
Total	3645	600	3020	25

Repair expenses apportioned to your personal unit are nondeductible personal expenses. Other expenses apportioned to personal use are deductible, provided your itemized deductions are in excess of your zero-bracket amount.

DEPRECIATION AFTER CONVERSION OF HOME TO RENTAL

If you convert your residence to a rental property, you can begin to take depreciation on the building. The amount of depreciation allowed is based on the lower of either the building's fair market value at the time of conversion or the adjusted cost basis (original purchase price plus improvements until time of conversion).

BASIS TO USE ON SALE OF A RENTAL PROPERTY

If you sell and realize a profit, you use the adjusted cost basis at the time of conversion less depreciation to determine your profit for tax purposes. If you sell at a loss, you use the lower of adjusted cost basis or fair market value at the time of conversion, less depreciation, to calculate the loss.

RULES FOR VACATION HOMES

For tax purposes, you should remember: (1) Mortgage interest is deductible only on first and second homes, capped at $1 million (1988 and after). (2) Deductible losses on rented vacation homes are limited to $25,000 (this cap is reduced when adjusted gross income is over $100,000).

The tax law prohibits most homeowners from deducting losses (expenses in excess of income) while renting out a personal vacation home. A vacation home can be a condominium, apartment, house trailer, motor home, boat, or house. Certain tests are formulated to disallow losses. These tests are based on the days of rental and personal usage. The following tests will determine whether you are allowed losses.

1. If the vacation home is rented for less than 15 days, you cannot deduct expenses allocated to the rental (except for interest and real estate taxes). If you sell and realize a profit on the rental, the profit is not taxable if the conditions for tax deferral or tax-free sale are met.
2. If the vacation home is rented for 15 days or more, you have to determine if your personal use of the home exceeds a 14-day or 10 percent time test (10 percent of the number of days the home is rented). If it does, then you are considered to have used the home as a residence during the year and rental expenses are deductible only to the extent of a gross rental income. Therefore, if gross rental income exceeds expenses, the operating gain is fully taxable.
3. If you rent the vacation home for 15 days or more, but your rental usage is less than the 14-day/10 percent test, then you are not considered to have made personal use of the residence during the year. In this case, expenses in excess of gross rental income may be deductible. Previous tax court cases have allowed loss deductions when the owner made little personal use of the

vacation home and proved to have bought the house to earn a profitable amount in resale.

RULES FOR THE HOME OFFICE

Keep in mind that: (1) Rental arrangements between employers and employees are disallowed. (2) Home-office deduction is limited to net income from trade or business. (3) Home-office deduction in excess of net income can be carried forward to future years.

In order to claim a deduction for a home office the office must be used exclusively and on a regular basis for an office (the room where your family watches television or reads while you work does not qualify). It must be used for actually meeting patients or customers (making phone calls to patients or customers won't qualify) or as the primary place of business. Taxpayers can operate more than one business for the purpose of this test, therefore employees can moonlight in another business and claim home-office deductions if the office is maintained for the convenience of the employer. An unattached structure used in connection with the taxpayer's business will also qualify.

According to the tax law, certain deductions are allowed for a home office, such as depreciation, insurance, utilities, and so on, that can offset income realized from the business. These deductions can only be claimed up to the net income of that business.

For example, an employee operates a separate home business as a writer. Earnings are $4400 in royalties during the year. Expenses for the year are postage and office supplies ($920), subscriptions ($1280), and depreciation on the home office ($90). Deductions for depreciation, insurance, and utilities can only be used to the extent of the net income of the home business determined without these items (see the example).

In the example, the taxpayer's deductions for a home office are limited to $2200. Home-office expenses cannot be used as a tax loss to offset other income. Although there is a total of $2690 in home-office expenses—depreciation ($2400) + utilities ($200) + insurance ($90)—

Royalties		$4400
Expenses other than home/office		
Postage and office supplies	$ 920	
Subscriptions	1280	
Subtotal		2200
Net income before home-office deductions		2200

there is $490 in unused deductions that can be carried forward and used against business income in future years.

Home-office expenses are considered a miscellaneous itemized deduction, which means they are subject to the same limitations imposed on all miscellaneous itemized deductions: A deduction can only be allowed when that total miscellaneous deduction exceeds 2 percent of the taxpayer's income.

RULES FOR DEPRECIATION

The main points are: (1) Residential rentals are depreciated over 27.5 years; commercial rentals over 31.5 years. (2) Only the straight-line method of depreciation is allowed on income property. (3) Vehicles are depreciated over five years. (4) Most machinery and equipment is depreciated over seven years. (5) Personal property is depreciated using the 200 percent declining-balance method.

Depreciation is the percentage reduction in loss of value of an asset over its physical life. It is strictly a bookkeeping entry, not an out-of-pocket expense to the investor.

Generally speaking, if you buy property to use in a trade or business or to earn rent or royalty income and the property has a useful life of more than one year, you cannot deduct its entire cost in one year. You must spread the cost over several years and deduct a part of it each year. For most types of property, this is called *depreciation*.

What Can Be Depreciated?

Many different kinds of property can be depreciated, such as machinery, buildings, vehicles, patents, copyrights, furniture, and equipment. Property is depreciable if it meets all three of these tests:

1. It must be used in business or held for the production of income (for example, to earn rent or royalty income).
2. It must have a useful life that can be determined and its useful life must be longer than one year. The useful life of a piece of property is an estimate of how long you can expect to use it in your business or to earn rent or royalty income from it.
3. It must be something that wears out, decays, gets used up, becomes obsolete, or loses value from natural causes.

Depreciable property may be tangible (that is, it can be seen or touched) or intangible. Intangible property includes such items as a copyright or franchise. Depreciable property may be personal or real. Personal property is property that is not real estate, such as machinery or equipment. Real property is land and generally anything that is erected on, growing on, or attached to land. However, the land itself is not depreciable.

Depreciation not only serves the purpose of determining taxable income but it is also the essence of why real estate has been a tax shelter. Historically real estate investors have been able to earn substantial net income free of taxes from their properties while actually showing taxable losses that could be written off against salary income. Thus the tax-shelter benefit of real estate, because the taxable loss (actually a net gain, or profit) can shelter salary income from other sources.

Figuring Depreciation

It is important to understand the two basic types of assets, each of which is depreciable under different rules. One can obtain valuable tax savings by carefully drawing distinctions between these two types of property because, although real property is limited to straight-line depreciation, personal property can be depreciated using accelerated methods of depreciation.

Depreciating Buildings

Residential real property is depreciated using the straight-line method (an equal amount of depreciation annually) over a useful life of 27.5 years (31.5 years for nonresidential property such as office buildings and shopping centers). In the month you purchase, or put the building in use, you are required to use one-half month's depreciation deduction. This is referred to as the *midmonth convention.*

Residential property is defined as a building with 80 percent or more of its rental income derived from dwelling units. A *dwelling unit* is defined as an apartment or house used to provide living accommodations. This does not include hotels or motels which rent more than half of their capacity on a temporary basis. If you reside in one of the apartments, a fair rental value can be allocated to your living unit.

Depreciating Land Improvements

Certain land improvements are depreciated over 15 years using the 150 percent declining-balance method. Conversion to the straight-line method at the time that maximizes deductions is also allowed. Depreciable land improvements are items such as bridges, roads, sidewalks, and landscaping. Sewer pipes are depreciated over a 20-year period. Buildings and their improvements are not allowed under this method.

Depreciating Equipment and Fixtures

Personal property, such as vehicles, equipment, or furniture, is generally written off by using the accelerated 200 percent declining-balance method over a five- or seven-year period. For example, most cars and light trucks are depreciated over five years. Most office furniture, fixtures, and equipment (desks, safes, and certain communication equipment) are depreciated over seven years. In addition, only one-half year of depreciation deduction is allowed in the year the asset was purchased or built (the *half-year convention*). The half-year convention also applies to real property. (Note that the accelerated methods of 150 percent and 200 percent declining balance are calculated at one and a half and twice, respectively, the rate of the straight-line method.) Table 19.2 illustrates how the declining-balance method works for five-year property.

The tax law permits a switch to the straight-line method when it will provide a larger deduction. In the fifth year the 200 percent declining-balance method would provide a deduction of $830 (40 percent × $2074). Switching to the straight-line method in the fifth year provides a deduction of $1382 ($2074 of costs not yet written off, divided by the 1.5 years remaining in the depreciation period). The half-year convention causes the depreciation period to be extended to a sixth year.

The calculations for seven-year property and the 150 percent declining-balance method of depreciation are similar, except that under

Table 19.2 Example of the 200 Percent Declining-Balance Method

Year	(Declining Balance) Cost	Rate of Depreciation %	Amount of Depreciation
1	$12,000	40 × .5	$2,400
2	9,600	40	3,840
3	5,760	40	2,304
4	3,456	40	1,382
5	2,074	—	1,382
6	692	—	692
			$12,000

the 150 percent method one and a half times the straight-line method is used (30 percent of 40 percent) in the depreciation-rate column.

"At-Risk" Rules

The latest tax law treats real estate the same as other investment activities. At-risk rules limit the amount of losses you can deduct. Specifically, these losses (deductions) cannot exceed the total of:

- The cash you contribute to the business.
- The adjusted basis of your property contributions to the business.
- The amount you borrowed for the business, but only to the extent you pledge other assets or have personal liability as security for the borrowing. The exception to this is financing secured only by the property itself, called "qualified nonrecourse financing." To qualify, the nonrecourse financing must be:
    - Secured only by the real property.
    - Actual debt (not disguised equity similar to convertible debt).
    - Obtained from a qualified lender, such as an institutional lender or related party. (If obtained from a related party, such as the seller or the promoter of the investment, the loan is required to be at reasonable market rates similar to those made to unrelated parties.)

RULES FOR PASSIVE INCOME AND LOSSES

The highlights to consider are: (1) Deductible losses on real estate are limited to $25,000, reduced for adjusted gross over $100,000. (2) Losses are not deductible under the $25,000 cap unless you actively participate in managing the property. (3) Losses in excess of $25,000 can be used only to offset gains from other passive investments.

A *passive activity* is any activity that involves the conduct of any trade or business in which you do not materially participate. *Any rental activity is a passive activity even if you materially participate in it.* A *trade* or *business* includes any activity involving research or experimentation and, to the extent provided in the regulations, any activity in connection with a trade or business or any activity for which a deduction is allowed as an expense for the production of income. You are considered to participate materially if you are in-

Table 19.3 Example of Three Types of Income for Passive-Loss Rules

Active	Passive	Portfolio
Employee wages	Most rental real estate	Interest
Primary trade or business	Net leased realty	Dividends
Real estate development	Limited partnership	REIT (Real Estate Investment Trust) distributions
Active retailer	No material participation	Royalties
Consultant		

volved in the operation of the activity on a regular, continuous, and substantial basis. Participation by your spouse will be considered in determining whether you materially participate.

For the tax years beginning after 1986, your deductions from passive activities may only be used to offset your income from passive activities. Any excess deductions result in a "passive-activity loss" and may not be deducted against your other income but may be carried over and applied against passive income in future years. In addition, any allowable credits from passive activity may only be used to offset future tax liability allocable to your passive activities.

These rules apply to any individual, estate, trust, closely held C corporation, or personal service corporation. They do not apply to any carryovers from a tax year beginning before 1987. Entities, such as partnerships and S corporations, must separately report their passive-activity items to their partners and shareholders so that they may properly reflect them on their 1988 tax return.

Now to illustrate the impact of the new passive-loss limitations compared to the old rules. For example, assume an investor with an aversion to paying income taxes has purchased real estate tax shelters in the past from a syndicator for the purpose of sheltering other income. Other sources of income are salary from a job as an executive of a corporation, dividends and interest, and investments in several tax shelters.

Salary	$150,000
Dividends	21,000
Interest	14,000
Tax-shelter losses	(183,000)
Taxable income before exemptions	$ 2,000

After taking into consideration the personal exemption, the investor in this example would in fact owe no tax. The income under passive-income rules falls into the three categories: Salary of $150,000 under the active income category, dividends and interest under the portfolio category, and tax shelter losses under the passive-income category.

Under the latest tax reform this investor will generally not be allowed to use the losses from the passive-income category to offset income and gains from the other categories. Therefore, under the latest reform provisions, the investor will no longer be able to avoid paying taxes. Total income will be $185,000 ($150,000 active income and $35,000 portfolio income), and in 1988 there will be a tax of $51,800 ($185,000 × 28 percent), overlooking standard deductions. This dramatic result is exactly what Congress sought to achieve when it made changes to investment taxation under the Tax Reform Act of 1986.

Certain Passive-Income Losses Can Offset Other Income

As mentioned before, an interest in real estate rental activity, no matter how much you participate, will not be considered an active business. This means that losses from real estate investments are only allowed to offset income and gains from other passive investments. Therefore, real estate losses cannot shelter wage or active business income. However, there is a major exception to this rule to assist moderate-income taxpayers who invest in real estate.

Certain investors can apply passive-income losses to wage earnings or income from an active business. In order to qualify for this real estate loss exception (up to a maximum of $25,000), the investor must meet both an income and a participation test. The investor's adjusted gross income must be less than $150,000. The entire $25,000 loss allowance is permitted for taxpayers with adjusted gross income up to $100,000. Over this amount, the allowance is reduced by 50 percent of the amount by which the adjusted gross income exceeds $100,000. Thus, if the adjusted gross income is $150,000, this allowance is zero.

The other requirement for this loss allowance is that the investor must "actively participate." (This rule is not so stringent as other participation tests, as you will soon see.) To get the benefit of up to $25,000 in tax losses, the investor is required to meet the following two tests: (1) The investor must own at least 10 percent of the value of the activity during the entire year that the allowance is claimed. (2) The investor is required to make management decisions or arrange for others to provide such services. It is not necessary for the investor to do certain things directly, such as repairs or approving prospective tenants. The hiring of a repair man and a rental agent does not violate the participation test; however, caution should be taken if you hire a management company to operate the property. The property management agreement should clearly indicate that you, the investor, are involved in the decision-making process.

Passive-Income Losses Are Carried Forward

Those losses the investor couldn't use during one tax year are carried forward as "suspended losses" and used in one of two ways: (1) If the investor has unused losses incurred in prior years and carried forward, those losses apply against income or gains in the passive-income category in future years. Under previous tax law the losses would have been used to shelter income from other sources. However, under current law they can only be used to shelter the income in later years for the same or other passive-income investments. (2) Unused suspended losses from prior years can be used to reduce any gain you realize when you dispose of your investment.

In determining income or loss from an activity, do not consider (A) any gross income from interest, dividends, annuities, or royalties not derived in the ordinary course of a trade or business; (B) expenses (other than interest) that are clearly and directly allocable to such other income; (C) interest expense properly allocable to such income; and (D) gain or loss from the disposition of property producing such income or held for investment. Any interest in a passive activity is not treated as property held for investment. In addition, you do not include wages, salaries, professional fees, or other amounts received as compensation for services rendered as income from a passive activity.

Rental Real Estate Activity

An individual will be allowed a deduction for any passive-activity loss or the deduction equivalent of the passive-activity credit for any tax year from rental real estate activities in which there is active participation. The amount allowed under this rule, however, cannot be more than $25,000 (or $12,500 for a married individual filing separately). This amount is reduced by 50 percent of the amount by which your adjusted gross income is more than $100,000 ($50,000 for married filing separately). Therefore, if your adjusted gross income exceeds $150,000 ($75,000 for married filing separately), this allowance rule does not apply.

Effective Dates of the New Passive-Loss Rules

Finally, you have to take into consideration when these new rules went into effect. Beginning in 1987, they are effective for all losses. However, for investments made prior to October 22, 1986, when the Tax Reform Act was enacted, these new rules are phased in over a five-year period. The following percentages of your losses are disallowed each year:

Year	Loss Disallowed (%)
1987	35
1988	60
1989	80
1990	90
1991 and after	100

Special care should be taken regarding the alternative minimum tax (AMT) because there is no phase-in of the passive-loss rules for the AMT. You may not get any immediate benefit from your passive losses if you're subject to the AMT. Furthermore, if you incurred passive losses before 1986 and passive gains after the tax reform, the profits on these latter investments must be netted against your passive losses before these phase-in rules can be used.

ALTERNATIVE MINIMUM TAX (AMT)

Because of the complexities of the new AMT, only a brief overview of it is given here. The subject of the AMT requires an accountant's attention to give you a thorough understanding of the law and to learn whether you qualify under its rules. Generally, only the wealthiest and the most heavily sheltered taxpayers have to concern themselves with the AMT.

Since 1986 taxpayers are subject to a 21 percent minimum tax, and computational changes and new concepts have also been introduced that further complicate what is complicated already.

For many years before the Tax Reform Act of 1986, Congress found it appropriate to encourage long-term investment in production facilities so as to improve the United States' competitive edge. One of the incentives used to promote this type of investment was the preferential treatment of capital gains, which allowed taxpayers to exclude 60 percent of any gain realized from the sale of an asset. This incentive to promote capital formation was a worthy goal, but so was tax equity. Therefore, in order to maintain a certain amount of fairness in the tax system, Congress decided that everyone should pay at least a minimum amount of tax, which resulted in the Alternative Minimum Tax. (For more information on the AMT for individuals, see Internal Revenue Service Publication 909, *Alternative Minimum Tax*.)

LONG-TERM CAPITAL GAINS

You should be aware that: (1) You can no longer exclude 60 percent of long-term capital gains. (2) Capital gains are taxed as ordinary income.

The preferential treatment of capital gains has traditionally been one of the most important benefits for real estate investors. Before the 1986 tax reform, capital gains rules allowed the taxpayer to exclude 60 percent of the gain realized on the sale of an asset for tax purposes. Under the new rules, capital gains benefits have been repealed, and all gains realized in the sale of an asset have to be taxed as regular income.

In addition, Congress changed the taxation on installment sales. An *installment sale* is one in which the seller takes back a mortgage and the buyer pays for the property over an extended term. Under the previous rules, the seller would report a portion of each payment received as profit subject to tax. New tax reform legislation has made a number of changes to this rule.

As mentioned before, the 60 percent exclusion afforded capital gains has been repealed. The new law incorporates a phase-in (transition period), setting five tax rates during the tax year 1987. All capital gains after 1987 will be taxed just like ordinary income once the new law is completely effective (see Table 19.4).

According to the new rules, an individual taxpayer's income will

Table 19.4 1988 and After Taxable Income Brackets

Tax Rate (%)	Married, Filing Joint Return	Married, Filing Separate Return	Heads of Household	Single Individuals
15	0–$29,750	0–$14,875	0–$23,900	0–$17,850
28	over $29,750	over $14,875	over $23,900	over $17,850

be grouped together and subject to the applicable tax rates. However, under a special rule, capital gains taxes were limited to a maximum rate of 28 percent during the transition year of 1987. Therefore, for the 1987 tax year ordinary income was taxed up to the rate of 38.5 percent, excluding capital gains, which was taxed at a maximum rate of 28 percent.

RULES FOR INSTALLMENT SALES

To understand the new rules for installment sales it is necessary to review prior rules (most of which are still applicable) from before tax reform. The intent of Congress in changing the tax laws was simplification; however, the actual result was to make the new rules more complex, especially in the area of the installment sale.

If you sell a real estate investment and realize the entire sales price in the year of the sale, the entire gain is taxable in the year the sale took place. An alternative to this is for the seller to accept a down payment and take back a purchase-money mortgage for the balance owing wherein the buyer would pay principal and interest on the unpaid balance over an extended period of time. This would be considered an installment sale.

How much of the deferred payments under an installment sale are taxable? The rules state that to determine the taxable amount of income on each payment, the gross profit ratio is applied to each payment received. The gross profit ratio is computed by dividing the taxable gain (gross profit) by the total sales price.

For example, you sell your residence that you paid \$50,000 for 10 years ago for \$200,000. You have a taxable gain of \$150,000 (\$200,000 sales price less the \$50,000 investment). The sales price of \$200,000 is the amount you will receive. What portion of each deferred payment do you report as income?

$$\text{Gross Profit Ratio} = \frac{\text{Taxable Gain (\$150,000)}}{\text{Total Sales Price (\$200,000)}} = 75\%$$

In this example, 75 percent of the down payment and of each additional deferred payment must be reported as income.

In the event the buyer in the above example were to assume an existing mortgage, the total sales price for the purpose of this calculation would be reduced by the amount of such mortgage. For example, the buyer assumes an existing mortgage of \$25,000 in addition to making deferred payments on a purchase-money mortgage to you. Therefore, the total sales price would be reduced by $25,000 and different gross profit calculations have to be made.

Total Sales Price	$200,000
Mortgage Assumed	25,000
Adjusted Sales Price	$175,000

Under these circumstances the portion of each payment that is considered is 85.71 percent ($150,000 taxable gain divided by the adjusted sales price of $175,000).

Borrowing Against Your Installment Notes

Up to this point, all the existing tax rules regarding installment sales are applicable to today's tax laws. New rules derived from 1986 tax reform apply to the disposition of funds acquired when an investor borrows against (uses as collateral) such installment notes. Before tax reform many taxpayers could obtain cash without triggering the unreported gain by pledging their installment notes as collateral for loans. For example, from the above illustration, you could have used the $150,000 notes as collateral for a loan up to this amount from an unrelated financial institution. Since the borrowing of funds would not have been treated as a sale of the notes, you could have obtained cash without triggering a gain on the installment notes.

Under tax reform the rules attempt to deny the availability of the installment-sale method to the extent of total borrowings through the new "proportionate disallowance rule." This rule tries to determine what portion of your total borrowings relate to the installment notes you're holding. Congress felt it appropriate since installment sales received fair treatment by taxation of only that part of the gain received each year. However, if you borrow against these deferred payments and now have all the cash, the tax deferred under the installment sale should be paid.

Because it is often difficult to determine which assets were pledged to support which liabilities, average figures are used to compute a ratio. In order to determine this average ratio, you divide applicable installment debt by your total assets and multiply the result by your average borrowings. The resulting percentage provides a rough estimate of how much of your borrowings are attributable to the installment notes you hold.

$$\frac{\text{Installment notes}}{\text{Total assets}} \times \text{Average borrowings} = \begin{array}{l}\text{Deemed payment on}\\ \text{installment obligations}\end{array}$$

Special Rules and Exceptions to the Installment Sale

First of all, the above-mentioned rules do not apply to the installment sale of your personal residence. Most farm property is also excluded.

The disposal of certain timeshare property and unimproved land is not subject to the proportionate disallowance rule if the buyer's obligation to repay the installment notes is not guaranteed or insured by a third party. In addition, neither the seller or any affiliates may develop the land. Because of this special treatment the seller is required to pay interest on the deferred tax liability. Sale of publicly traded property, such as REITs, cannot be reported under the installment method.

Property subject to the passive-loss limitation rules sold under the installment method require particular attention. The suspended passive losses (the unused portion) will be recognized in each year in the ratio of the profit realized in that year to the total profit to be realized on that transaction. In order to trigger realization of the entire loss in the year of the sale you must elect not to have the installment-sales rules apply.

In conclusion, a major change is the prohibition of the use of the installment-sale method altogether if one elects to use the alternative minimum tax. This applies to anyone subject to the proportionate disallowance rule and includes investors involved with residential subdividing, the sale of real estate used in trade or business, and rental real estate where the purchase price exceeds $150,000. Under these circumstances, especially if you're subject to the alternative minimum tax, an installment sale will not benefit you. It is therefore recommended that you structure your real estate sales so that you realize enough cash in the year of the sale to pay any tax due.

TAX CREDITS FOR LOW-INCOME HOUSING AND REHABILITATION

Highlights of the current tax laws are: (1) Low-income housing credit is 9 percent of construction cost or 4 percent of the acquisition cost. (2) Credit is reduced to 10 percent for non-CHS (Certified Historical Structure) structures built before 1936, 20 percent for CHS. (3) Investment tax credit is repealed.

New Tax Credit for Low-Income Rental Housing

Tax reform has created new incentives based on a two-tier tax credit for encouraging the construction or rehabilitation of low-income rental housing. The two-tier credit system offers a different tax credit for different types of qualifying expenditures. A 9 percent tax credit is available for new construction and rehabilitation expenditures placed in service in 1987. A 4 percent tax credit is available for the cost of acquiring an existing building in 1987 or new or existing construction which is financed with federal subsidies. Each tax credit is available every year for 10 years. After 1987, the structure of the tax credits will remain generally the same. However, each tax credit rate will be revised by the IRS on a monthly basis in order to reflect changes in market interest rates.

As an example of the tax-credit savings available, consider the following: Over 10 years on a $100,000 qualifying expenditure, you could generate $9000 (or $4000) in credit annually for 10 years, or a sum of $90,000 (or $40,000).

How to Qualify. Certain requirements must be met to qualify for the low-income housing credit.

1. A minimum portion of the building must be reserved for use by low-income families. This can be achieved in one of two ways, and the owner must irrevocably select which of the two will be used. The first test to qualify requires that 20 percent or more of the entire project be occupied by families or individuals having incomes no greater than one-half that of the median-income level for that area. The second test requires that 40 percent or more of the entire project be occupied by families or individuals with incomes no more than 60 percent of the median income for that area.
2. The available units must be suitable and be used for occupancy on a nontransient basis.
3. The gross rent paid by the low-income family or individual cannot be more than 30 percent of the qualifying income level for that family or individual. This rental figure includes the cost of utilities, except telephone, in order to qualify.
4. The owner of a low-income project is required to certify to the IRS that, in fact, the project has complied with the various requirements.
5. The project must meet these requirements for a compliance period of 15 years to qualify for the low-income housing credit. If during the compliance period, requirements are not met, then a portion of the credit will have to be recaptured (given back), which will increase the tax liability.

Figuring the Tax Credit. The following is the general formula used to figure the low-income housing tax credit:

> Cost of construction or purchase (eligible basis) × Proportion of eligible basis attributable to low-income units = Qualified basis × Credit percentage of 9% or 4% in 1987 = Low-income housing tax credit

The eligible basis of the formula consists of three components that determine the amount of expenditures that qualify for the tax credit:

1. The cost of eligible construction.
2. The cost of rehabilitation expenditures. To qualify these expenditures must average at least $2000 per low-income housing unit. Cost incurred for rehabilitation during a two-year period from the date the rehabilitation originated can be included.
3. The cost of acquiring an existing project. For the costs of an existing project to qualify in the eligible basis, the project and any improvement to it had to have been put into service more than 10 years before the current acquisition. The costs of any rehabilitation expenditures incurred before the end of the first year of the credit period can be included. Minimum rehabilitation expenditures, as described in item 2, are not required.

Certain general requirements apply to the eligible expenditures in the above three items. The investment, or tax basis, of the project is included in the amount, but the cost of the land is not. Should the investor claim the rehabilitation tax credit, a reduction in the depreciable basis of the project is factored into the calculation of eligible basis. Expenditures for certain personal property, such as furniture and fixtures, can be included. The cost of certain tenant facilities can also be included in the eligible basis if no separate fee is charged and the facilities are made available on a comparable basis for all tenants. These include facilities such as parking lots, swimming pools, tennis courts, or other recreational areas. If there are commercial tenants in the project, it will be considered eligible. However, the cost of such nonresidential activity is required to be excluded from the eligible basis calculation. Finally, no portion of the funds derived from any federal grant can be included in the eligible basis.

To determine the proportion of the eligible basis that can be included in the amount (qualifying basis) on which the low-income credit is calculated multiplying the eligible basis by the lower of the two ratios below:

$$\frac{\text{Total number of low-income units}}{\text{Total number of residential units}}$$

or

$$\frac{\text{Floor space of low-income units}}{\text{Total floor space of residential units}}$$

In figuring the floor space ratios you can only use low-income units that are actually occupied by low-income tenants. The figure for total number of residential units, on the other hand, includes all units, whether they are occupied or not.

In conclusion, before being overwhelmed by the benefits of such a tax credit, carefully consider the limitations, restrictions, and, of course, the cumbersome red tape involved. In many cases the tax credit for low-income housing will not be available or, if available, will not be worth the bother.

Tax Credit for Rehabilitating Old and Historic Buildings

Tax reform has substantially reduced the benefits and availability of the tax credit associated with renovating certain old and/or historic buildings. Although these new rules are more restrictive, the tax credit deserves attention because it can be valuable to real estate developers in some situations. Essentially, the tax credit is a two-tier credit that can offset you tax liability on a dollar-for-dollar basis, as follows:

1. Twenty percent tax credit on costs incurred in renovating a building that qualifies as a certified historic structure. For the building to qualify it must be located in a registered historic district or be listed in the National Register of Historic Places. In addition, the Secretary of the Interior must approve the renovation of the building.
2. Ten percent tax credit on costs incurred in renovating a building that was placed in service before 1936. Only residential property may qualify for the 20 percent certified historic-structure credit. It may or may not qualify for the 10 percent credit. To qualify for the tax credit the renovation must be "substantial." This means that the qualifying cost spent on the renovation work itself, exclusive of the acquisition costs of building and land or enlarging the building, must be greater than (1) \$5000 or (2) your investment (adjusted tax basis, which is cost less depreciation) in the building. These renovations must be completed within 24 months. (This qualifying period can be extended under certain circumstances.)

In addition to the above requirements, certain other tests must be met:

- At least 75 percent of the structure's external walls must be retained as either external or internal walls.
- At least 75 percent of the building's internal structural framework, such as beams and load-bearing walls, must be retained.
- At least 50 percent of the structure's external walls must be retained as external walls.

If you claim the tax credit, the adjusted tax basis of the building must be reduced by the amount of the tax credit in calculating depreciation. Finally, if the owner of the renovated building agrees, the rehabilitation tax credit can be claimed by the building's tenant. For the tenant to qualify, the unexpired lease term must at least equal the depreciation period for the property, which is 27.5 years for residential property and 31.5 years for nonresidential property.

MISCELLANEOUS TAX AND ADMINISTRATIVE CHANGES

Tax reform has brought about numerous administrative and technical changes relevant to the real estate industry. The intent of this section is to make you aware of these changes, enabling you to work or communicate more efficiently with your tax advisor.

Registration of Tax Shelters

A tax shelter must be registered with the IRS, and the registration must be no later than the day on which interests in it are first offered for sale to the investors. The principal organizer of the shelter is responsible for the filing. However, if this person fails to do so, another member of the shelter can be responsible.

An investment is considered a tax shelter for registration requirements if the investment's tax shelter ratio for any of the first five years of the investment is greater than 2:1.

$$\frac{\text{Total deductions} + (350\% \times \text{tax credits})}{\text{Investment}}$$

If this ratio is more than 2:1, the investment qualifies.

In addition to the above ratio requirement, the investment is required (1) to be registered under a federal or state law regulating securities; (2) to be more than, in aggregate, $250,000 and sold to at least five or more investors; or (3) to be sold pursuant to an exemption for registration requiring the filing of a notice with a federal or state agency.

Under registration requirements the seller must provide each investor with the tax shelter identification number issued by the IRS and this number must be reported on the tax return.

Finally, the IRS can assess penalties for failing to meet these requirements:

- A 1 percent penalty, or $500, whichever is greater, can be assessed for failing to register a tax shelter.
- A $250 penalty can be assessed for failing to report the tax shelter identification number on a tax return.
- The tax shelter organizer can be assessed a penalty of $50 per failure up to a maximum of $100,000 per year for failing to maintain an investor list.

Reporting Rental Income and Deductions

Rental income and expenses are reported on Schedule E of your tax return. You report the gross amount received, then deduct such expenses as mortgage interest, property taxes, maintenance costs, and depreciation. The net profit is added to your other taxable income. If you realize a loss, you can reduce the amount of your other taxable income within certain limitations. (See passive-loss limitation rules in this section.)

If the cash basis is used as the accounting method, you report rental income for the year in which you receive payment. On the accrual basis, you report rental income for the year in which you are entitled to receive payment. You do not report accrued income if the financial condition of your tenant makes collection doubtful. If you sue for payment, you do not report income until you win a collectible judgment. Insurance proceeds for loss of rental income because of fire or casualty loss are reported as ordinary income. Payment by a tenant for cancelling a lease or modifying its terms is reported as ordinary income when received. You may deduct expenses realized from the cancellation and any unamortized balance for expenses paid in negotiating the lease. Security deposits are treated as trust funds and are not reported as income. However, if your tenant breaches the lease agreement, then you are entitled to use the security deposit as rent, at which time you report it as income.

CHECKLIST OF DEDUCTIONS FROM RENTAL INCOME

Real Estate Taxes. Property taxes are deductible, but special assessments for paving roads, sewers, or other improvements are not. They are added to the cost of the land.

Depreciation. Be sure to deduct depreciation on income property; it is the tax shelter benefit of real estate ownership.

Maintenance Expenses. Repairs, pool service, heating, lighting, water, gas, electricity, telephone, and other service costs.

Management Expenses. Include the cost of stationery and postage stamps or the total cost of a management service.

Traveling Expenses. These include travel back and forth from properties for repairs, rent collection, or showing vacancies.

Legal Expenses. These include the costs incurred while evicting a tenant. Expenses incurred for negotiating long-term leases are considered capital expenditures and are deductible over the term of the lease.

Interest Expense. This includes interest on mortgages and other indebtedness related to the property.

Advertising Expense. This includes the cost of vacancy signs and newspaper advertising.

Insurance Expense. This includes the cost of premiums for fire and casualty loss.

Note the difference between repair expenses and an improvement. Only incidental repair and maintenance costs are deductible against rental income. Improvement and replacement costs are treated differently. Improvements or repairs that add value or prolong the life of the property are considered capital improvements and may not be deducted but may be added to the cost basis of the property and then be depreciated. For example, the cost to repair the roof of a rental property is considered an expense and is deducted against rental income. However, the cost to replace the entire roof is considered an improvement (it adds value and prolongs the physical life of the property) and is therefore added to the cost basis of the property and then depreciated.

SUMMARY

Congress designed the 1986 Tax Reform Act with the intention of implementing a doctrine of fairness, and at the same time it attempted to simplify the overall tax system. It did accomplish a certain amount of fairness when it reduced individual tax rates and strictly limited the amount of tax shelter benefits, especially for the very wealthy. However, it did not by any means simplify the tax system. In fact it has been made more complex.

Under the new regulations, special care must be taken by borrowers. Deductions for interest paid on loans other than mortgages depend upon how the borrowed money is used. Under the old law interest was generally deductible no matter how the proceeds from a loan were spent.

Since the 1986 Act taxpayers who borrow must trace how they use the loan proceeds from the day they take it out until the day it is repaid.

Under the new rules, more forms and stricter accounting practices are required of the taxpayer. In order to comply under the new complex system, the following procedures are suggested to simplify record-keeping and to avoid losing deductions because of improper record-keeping methods:

- Maintain separate accounts for personal, business, and investment use.
- Be sure that debts incurred for investments can be traced to the investment. (Note the 15-day rule that the taxpayer who spends the proceeds of a loan within 15 days qualifies for the deduction; however, if the loan proceeds sit longer than 15 days, the IRS will base the deduction eligibility on the first purchase made from the borrowed funds.)
- As opposed to other forms of loans, consider home-equity loans, which are fully tax deductible and don't require as much record-keeping.
- Refrain from writing checks on stock margin accounts for purposes other than buying stock.

20 SELLING YOUR PROPERTY

Although selling your property is a bit off the subject of real estate loans, it is closely related and information about it can be helpful; thus, this chapter is included.

Throughout the United States, two-thirds of the residential real estate is sold using the services of a broker; the remainder is sold by individual owners. The broker's fee for selling your home is usually 6 percent of the selling price. In return, the broker assists you in determining the right selling price, shows the home to prospective buyers, and lists it with the Multiple Listing Service (MLS). Listing with the MLS substantially expands the market for potential buyers, because brokers and agents from other offices are made aware of your listing through the MLS, and they likewise inform their buyers of your available property.

Besides showing the property, the listing agent is also helpful at closing the sale. In many cases the broker can act as the liaison between you and the buyer, working out any difficulties that may arise.

However, should you decide to save the sales commission and sell the property yourself, keep in mind that, on average, it takes 87 days to sell a home. This shows that it is by no means an easy task. Much preparation is required to do the job right. If you're prepared to invest the time and effort necessary to sell your own property and save the 6 percent commission, go right ahead. The following material is a step-by-step guide to accomplishing this.

TIMING THE SALE

Traditionally there are good times during the year to sell residential property as well as good times to buy. Good times to sell are during the spring and fall, primarily because it is then that most buyers are looking for property, especially if they have children attending school. Probably the worst time of the year to sell property is during the winter, especially at Christmas. During the holiday times, potential buyers are usually too occupied with other things to concern themselves with the purchase of a home. Conversely, since during this time there is a deficiency of buyers, this time of the year is the best time to make your purchase.

PRICE IT RIGHT

To establish the right price, it is first necessary to establish the least you'll accept in price. Then you can adjust your price upward from this point, allowing a little room for price negotiations. Most buyers like to negotiate, so allow yourself a little flexibility.

NECESSARY DOCUMENTS AND INFORMATION

After you decide what price to ask for the property, you can start gathering the documents and information you will need to consummate the sale.

You will need the following information from the loan documents:

- Is there a prepayment penalty on the first mortgage and, if so, will they waive it if the buyer obtains his mortgage from the same lender?
- What is the current principal balance owing on the loan?
- Is there a tax and insurance impound account and, if so, what is the balance in that account.

Note that the prepayment penalty is a cost to you, levied by the lender according to the original loan agreement, charging you a penalty (six months' interest on the unpaid balance is common) for repaying the loan before it's due. This penalty charge covers the lender's cost in reclaiming and then reloaning the money which you paid back prematurely and it may be waived, as mentioned earlier.

You will also need the following documents:

- A copy of the paid tax receipt for the previous year.
- A copy of the survey of your property.
- Evidence of title.

HOME-SELLING TIPS

Whether or not you use the services of a broker, it is still necessary to prepare the entire property for its eventual sale. The following material is a guide to preparation in order to get a quick and bona fide offer on your property.

Realtors use the phrases "this property has good curb appeal" (that is, it looks appealing at first sight) or "this house shows well" when showing homes to prospective buyers. This descriptive jargon is relevant to selling your home, because in order to get the best price for your home it is wise to prepare it to look its best.

Unless you want to sell a fixer-upper, or one that looks like a fixer-upper, one is required to put the house and the surrounding grounds in order so as to get the most out of it. Some of the preparation for the sale can simply be tidying up around the exterior of the house. But, unless you're an extremely tidy housekeeper, which most of us are not, you'll have to do some minor repair and touch-ups to meet good condition standards. Remember, anything in obvious disrepair will eventually be discounted from the offer price.

First impressions are most important. If the house doesn't look appealing from the curb, the prospective buyer might not consider getting out of the car to look further. The following are suggestions that will eventually assist in the quick sale of your home and will get the prospect out of the car and into your home for a further inspection.

Exterior

Tidy up all around the exterior grounds by removing any debris, old cars, and so on. Cut the grass and trim the hedges and shrubs. Neatly arrange and organize items such as outdoor furniture and firewood.

Store or have removed from the property items such as broken-down dishwashers, water heaters, or water softeners. (Avoid the look of a junkyard.)

Give the lawn a thorough raking and sweep the sidewalk and driveway.

Tour the perimeter of your property and repair any broken fencing and paint or stain areas that need attention.

Carefully inspect your front door. It's one of the first items your home-hunting prospects will examine. If it shows signs of wear, give it a fresh coat of paint or stain. While you are at it, spruce up the house numbers either with a touch-up paint job or replace with new shiny brass ones.

Quite often repainting the entire exterior of the house isn't necessary; you can substantially improve the appearance by repainting all the trim.

Repair any broken windows or screens, then wash them for a brighter appearance.

Interior

When you're finished with the exterior, start on the interior of your home. The objective here is to make your home look organized and spacious, bright, warm, and comfortable. I can't emphasize cleanliness enough. Now would be a good time for a thorough spring cleaning. A clean house will sell much faster than a dirty one.

Brighten dull rooms with a fresh coat of white, beige, or antique white paint. Lighter colors make rooms appear bigger and brighter, and neutral colors will go better with the new buyer's furnishings. Instead of taking the time and effort of pulling down old wallpaper and putting up new, try sprucing up the trim instead.

Rooms with too much furniture show very poorly. Prospective buyers require lots of room and that's what they're looking for. Rearrange your furniture to make rooms appear more spacious. Put excessive furniture in storage, then rearrange and organize what's left. You'll be surprised how much unwanted stuff can accumulate over the years.

Now have a giant garage sale to clear out all your unwanted stuff. You can earn extra money to spend on whatever, and you won't have to pay the movers to relocate all those unwanted items.

Clean all windows and mirrors.

If the carpet is dirty, have it professionally cleaned. If the carpet appears overly worn, consider having it replaced. It is unlikely you will recover the cost of a new carpet in the sale of your home, but most likely it will sell faster.

Clear kitchen counters to make your kitchen appear more organized and spacious. Clean and polish all appliances in the kitchen. Finish in the kitchen by making the sink shiny and sparkling.

Clean and shine the tub, toilet, and sink in all bathrooms.

Break out the tool box and start fixing all those little things you've been putting up with all these months. You know, the leaky faucet, loose door knobs, cracked receptacle and switch covers. Secure those loose moldings and towel racks and anything that wobbles.

These are all little items of disrepair that can detract from the beauty and function of your home. When a prospective buyer begins examining your home during a walk-through, he or she is mentally keeping track of any shortcomings. Too many little things in disrepair will bring a lower offer—if any at all—than if the house were in excellent condition.

When it's finally time to show your home to prospective buyers, all the preparations you made will definitely be worth the effort; your home will receive more and better offers than if you were ill-prepared for the sale. But there are a few additional items you should do just before you show the home that will add that little extra touch of comfort and hominess.

Just before your prospective buyers arrive, clear out the kids and secure the pets where they won't cause any distraction. Turn off the television and put on some soft music. Turn on all the lights in the house to make it as bright as possible, even during the daytime. If you have a fireplace, fire it up also. Liven up the aroma in your home with freshly baked cinnamon rolls right out of the oven. Finish up with clean towels on the racks and put out some fresh flowers to treat yourself for making your home such a tidy showplace.

When the prospects arrive, make yourself scarce (only when using a broker, that is). Your absence will make potential buyers more at ease. Your presence will only distract from the job at hand, that of looking over your entire home and answering any questions, which is the agent's responsibility. If you must be there, try to avoid any conversation with the prospects because the agent needs their full attention to stimulate interest in the features of your home.

Do not complicate the sale of your home by discussing the separate sale of certain appliances or the fact that you wish to keep certain personal items. Personal property, such as furniture and unattached appliances, can be negotiated later, at a more appropriate time.

Always maintain your home in a showplace condition, as you never know when just the right prospect might show up. Your agent will usually make appointments with you for showings, but if casual browsers drop in for an unexpected visit, it is best not to show your home. Ask for their name and phone number and refer the information to your agent.

Keep in mind that it takes time to sell a home. Be patient. Keep your home on the market for as long as it takes. Your home requires adequate exposure to enough prospective buyers in order to consummate a proper sale.

In closing, you might consider offering a one-year home warranty plan, which would offer a little more added value and overcome questions about the working order of major home systems. These policies are available through most national real estate brokerage companies and protect your buyers for one year against most major repairs.

PROPERTY INFORMATION SHEET

The property information sheet is only necessary if you plan to sell the property yourself. It is a list of all the vital measurements and other information about your home that you will distribute to prospective buyers. Use a 50-foot or longer tape measure to measure each room and do this as accurately as you can. Enter this and all other

Address ______________________ Selling Price $__________
____

Existing first mortgage balance __________ at ______ %
Existing second mortgage balance __________ at ______ %
Monthly payments on first $ ______ plus taxes and insurance $ ______
Monthly payments on second $______
Architectual style: __________ Const. __________ Basmt: __________

LR __________	Age: __________	Heat: __________
DR __________	Lot Size: __________	Air cond. __________
Kit __________	Garage: __________	220 Wiring: __________
Dinette: __________	Curbs & gut. __________	Water htr: __________
Fam. rm. __________	Paved st. __________	Water soft: __________
Other rm. __________	Sidewalk: __________	
Bath: __________	Water: __________	
Bath: __________	Sewer: __________	
Bath: __________	Septic: __________	
BR: __________		
BR: __________	Schools: High __________	Grade: ______
BR: __________	Middle __________	
BR: __________		

Draperies and curtains: __________
Carpeting: __________
Items included: Oven __________ Range __________ Frig __________
TV antenna __________ Disposal __________ Dishwasher __________
Items not included: ______________________________
____
Owner ______________________ Phone __________

Figure 20.1. Property information sheet

stipulated information on the sheet (see Figure 20.1) and make copies for distribution.

OPEN HOUSE AND THE FOR SALE SIGN

Traditionally, real estate agents hold open house on their listed properties mostly over weekends when the majority of potential buyers have the time off from work and can easily go house-hunting.

If you plan to sell your home yourself, weekends would also be the best time to hold your open house. If by chance other owners are holding open house during the same time as yours, you will actually benefit from it. Numerous open houses in the same neighborhood mean more prospective buyers will have the opportunity to see your property.

Unless your property is located on a well-traveled thoroughfare, you'll need several open-house signs to direct prospects to your property. Count the number of turns a prospect has to make from a major thoroughfare in order to get to your property. That will be the number of signs you'll need.

Your open-house signs should be 24 inches square with red letters on a white background. Each sign should read OPEN HOUSE with the appropriate address below and a red arrow pointing in the correct direction.

The sign in your front yard should read FOR SALE BY OWNER in red with your phone number below. In addition to the for sale sign, consider placing small pennants or flags near the street; these are excellent for arousing attention to your sale.

ADVERTISING

The purpose of your advertising is to get prospects interested enough in your property to come by and look for themselves. Place your ad in the classified section of your Sunday newspaper, because Sundays are when realtors place their ads. Prospective buyers are accustomed to looking for homes in the Sunday paper.

In addition, consider placing an ad for your open house in the Sunday paper. Most newspapers have a separate section classified under "Open House."

THE SALES AGREEMENT

At this point your property, both inside and out, is tidy and in complete repair. Your advertisements are running and the phone is ringing off the hook with inquiries about your property. Prospective buyers have been walking through your home day after day, and, finally, somebody says they're interested in purchasing your home or that they wish to sit down and discuss terms of the sale at your earliest convenience. What you have now is not a sale, but a serious and interested prospect. It is now time to negotiate and put the details of your negotiation into writing.

Once all the details of price and terms are agreed upon between you and the buyer, you will complete the purchase agreement checklist (see Figure 20.2). This checklist is used as a guideline in the preparation of documents for completion of sale. Either your escrow agent or an attorney can use this information and avoid having to spend time asking questions.

QUALIFYING THE BUYER

Just because you have a prospect who has announced readiness to purchase your home, this does not mean that you have a bona fide sale. Many a hopeful buyer may nevertheless lack the adequate income or the credit worthiness to attain financing, in which case it is futile to enter into a sales agreement.

If new financing is to be originated and the buyer has already arranged it or a lender has already tentatively approved a mortgage loan in your price range, then it is not necessary to qualify the buyer beyond getting proof of the above. In all other cases (loan assumption or a wrap-around loan), you must obtain certain information and qualify the buyer yourself. (For additional information on qualifying the buyer, see appropriate section on qualification procedures in Chapter 2.)

SUMMARY

We can now compare the total cost of selling the property yourself with the cost of having the same property sold by a real estate broker who receives a 6 percent commission. Assuming a $80,000 selling price, the broker's commission would be $4800 ($80,000 × 6%).

NOTE: This is not a legally binding agreement. It is simply a checklist to accommodate the drafting of a formal sales agreement between buyer and seller.

Name of prospective buyer(s) ______________________________
____
____

currently residing at ______________________________
______________________________ phone ______________
____

are considering purchasing the property located at ______________
____
____

for a purchase price of $ ______________

Earnest money deposit of $ ______________ to be held in escrow by ______________________________

Buyer to assume existing loans $ ______________

Or, buyer to originate new financing of $ ______________
____

Real estate taxes last year were ______________________________

Contingencies to be included in purchase agreement ______________
____
____
____
____

Items not included in selling price ______________________________
____
____

Items that are included in selling price ______________________________
____
____

Sellers will vacate the premises on ______________________________
____
____

Date of closing escrow ______________

Sellers to pay rent of $ ______________ per day if sellers occupy premises after the close of escrow.

Legal description of property ______________________________
____

Figure 20.2. Purchase agreement checklist

When you deduct your own costs of sale from this amount, that is your savings.

The following are approximate costs you incur in selling the property yourself, not including normal closing costs which have to be paid regardless of whether you use a broker.

For Sale signs	$ 60
Advertising	100
Copies of information sheet	5
Total cost	$165

Thus, you will make $4635 ($4800 − $165) or save that much, if you look at it that way, by selling the house yourself.

21 HOME INSPECTION CHECKLIST

Before going ahead with such a major purchase as a home, consider hiring a home inspector to uncover potential costly problems; you could save thousands of dollars on the price of the home. Listed in the Yellow Pages, a professional home inspector licensed by the American Society of Home Inspectors (ASHI) charges $125 to $250, depending on location.

Once you've found a home that you're interested in buying, you could make the offer contingent upon your approval of a home inspection by an independent contractor. The following is what you and the inspector should look for:

Electrical. Newer homes have a minimum 100 ampere service, which is adequate to handle modern appliances (microwave ovens, dishwashers, and clothes dryers). Older homes usually are equipped with a 60 ampere service, which could be adequate if the clothes dryer, range, and furnace operate on gas. In addition, rooms with only one electrical outlet are underserved. The cost of replacing 60 ampere service with a new 100 amp service is $300 to $700. The cost to install a new receptacle and wiring is about $35.

Interior Plumbing. Turn on the water and begin looking for leaks. Check for stained ceilings, drips under sinks, leaks around toilets while flushing, and puddles in the basement. Older homes may have galvanized steel pipes (check by using a magnet; they are gray in color) or brass pipes, either of which will eventually have to be replaced. Newer plumbing systems shouldn't give you any trouble. The cost of replacing the old plumbing can be $1000 or more, depending on the complexity of the house.

Roof. On shingled roofs, look for missing or curled shingles as evidence that a new roof is needed. On asphalt roofs, if the granular composition surface is worn off or stains are present on the underside of the overhang, it won't be long before a new roof is needed. Asphalt or shingle roofs on the average-size home cost about $1000 to be replaced and last about 20 years. The more expensive clay tile or wood shingle roofs cost about $2000 and may last 40 years.

Air Conditioning. Check the compressor to see whether it's running smoothly. The large intake pipe should cool quickly after the unit is turned on. If it doesn't, you could have a freon leak.

Heating. Be sure each room has a heating outlet.

Walls and Windows. In colder climates, look for storm windows. Cracked plaster is common in older homes; however, in newer homes it means the house is settling. Look for deteriorated caulking around windowsills and window frames; it will allow heat loss.

Foundations, Basements, and Underflooring. Evidence of previous water leaks or flooding are water stains on the basement walls and floor. Also look for white dust, which is a residue of salts washed out of the concrete. Because of the instability of the underlying earth, Florida homes should be checked to be sure the concrete slab is supported by pilings. Saggy or squeaky floors can be checked by examining the floor trusses underneath.

Termites. Tunnels in the wood are signs of termites. These wood-munching insects are primarily a problem in California, the Midwest and some southern states.

Septic Tanks and Wells. You can tell if the septic tank is functioning properly by mixing dye with running water. If the colored dye bubbles to the surface of the ground, the septic system will have to be replaced. If the house is on well water, run the water for an hour during the inspection. If the water runs dry, the yield is too low, which will require careful water conservation by your family if you decide to purchase this home.

22 ANSWERS TO COMMONLY ASKED QUESTIONS ABOUT REAL ESTATE LOANS

Selected topical questions and answers about real estate loans are featured in the following material.

DELINQUENT PAYMENTS

I noticed in my mortgage coupon that the due date of the payment is the first of the month; however, the lender doesn't charge a penalty unless the payment is made after the fifteenth of the month. Traditionally, I have paid the mortgage payment on the tenth and, as far as I can remember, I have not been assessed a late charge. Since my husband and I are planning to buy a new home, will our lender consider us late payers? And, if so, will it affect our ability to get a new loan?

No, don't worry about it. Your lender probably wishes he had more customers like you in the first place. If you studied your mortgage agreement, you would find that you actually have a grace period of 15 days during which the payment can be made without being considered delinquent. Sure, the lender would prefer to have your payment on the first, but getting it by the fifteenth is much better than perhaps 10 percent of the borrowers being chronically late and another 2 percent of them 30 days or more in arrears (when a loan is really considered to be delinquent). Only those payments that incurred a late payment will actually show up on the lender's record with a black mark. Since you always made the payment before the late-pay date, your loan record should be clean.

FIXED-RATE OR ARM?

Should I take out a mortgage now or wait until interest rates go lower? Also, which is better—the fixed-rate or adjustable-rate mortgage?

In reply to the first question, there is no telling exactly when rates will go up or down. As a rule, however, interest rates are either in a rising or falling trend, seldom are they stable. Once the initial direction changes, they will usually continue in that direction for a while until a new trend develops. Therefore, if interest rates are rising, it would be an educated gamble that, if you waited, you would pay more for a loan. On the other hand, if rates were falling, it would be likely that a cheaper rate could be attained if you waited.

Regarding the question as to which is better—a fixed rate mortgage or the ARM—it essentially depends on how long you plan to keep the mortgage. Both types of loans have inherent advantages and disadvantages.

As a rule, if you plan to own the property four years or less, then the ARM will be more economical. If you own the property more than four years, then the fixed-rate mortgage will cost you less. This is primarily due to lower initial rates on the ARM that in time gradually reach and surpass the rate of the fixed-rate mortgage.

Bear in mind that ARMs shift the risk of increasing interest rates from the lender to the borrower. In return, the borrower has certain caps that give protection against drastically increasing rates. More important, the ARM is assumable whereas most fixed-rate mortgages are not. This assumability is advantageous because this added flexibility makes your property more saleable.

SHOPPING FOR A LOAN

Most institutional lenders seem to be very competitive. Are all their rates the same? If not, how much can I save by shopping around?

Studies have shown that a homeowner could save $30,000 or more over the life of a typical mortgage if that person is an informed borrower. Rates can vary substantially among institutional lenders, and the educated borrower can save plenty of money if the correct decision is made. Like supermarkets, department stores, and other competing businesses, lenders charge different amounts for the same thing. Lenders have different costs and desired profit margins. In addition, they attempt to establish different customer bases. Thus, lenders' offerings can differ in both rates and origination fees.

INTEREST RATES AND BONDS

I was told that the value of municipal bonds goes down when interest rates go up. This doesn't seem logical to me. Would you clarify?

That's correct. Bond values rise when interest rates go down and, conversely, drop when interest rates go up. Let's say you own an 8 percent municipal bond issued by the township of Lansing with a face value of $5000 due to mature in 2001. Until maturity you collect $400 a year in interest. At maturity you will be paid $5000, unless Lansing defaults on its debt. Later, Lansing township issues more bonds on which it has to pay 10 percent interest because interest rates are higher than at the time your bond was issued. Now, in the open marketplace, the value of your bonds, the Lansing 8 percents, have dropped because an investor could now buy Lansing 10 percents for $5000 and earn $500. Why would an investor pay $5000 for your bond when he can pay the same amount of money and earn 10 percent? If interest rates drop, the same forces increase the value of bonds.

This inverse relationship applies to all types of bonds, including corporate bonds issued by companies and U.S. Treasury securities issued by Uncle Sam.

23 ANSWERS TO COMMONLY ASKED QUESTIONS ABOUT INCOME TAXES AND REAL ESTATE

The following material attempts to answer important topical questions regarding income taxes in relation to real estate.

DEDUCTIBLE INTEREST

When is mortgage interest deductible?

Interest on your principal residence or a second home is 100 percent deductible. Mortgage interest deductibility doesn't become questionable unless you refinance your home or take out a second mortgage.

LIMITS ON INTEREST DEDUCTIONS

What are the limitations on the mortgage interest deduction?

Mortgage debt incurred on or after October 14, 1987, is divided into two kinds of indebtedness, each with a separate limit. The first is "acquisition indebtedness" that is used to acquire or substantially improve a residence and is limited in tax year 1988 to $1 million for up to two residences. The other is "home equity indebtedness," which is any debt other than acquisition indebtedness secured by one or two residences. In the tax year 1988, the deduction is limited to the fair market value of the residence plus improvements, not to exceed $100,000.

All mortgage interest incurred on or before October 13, 1987, regardless of amount or purpose, is *grandfathered*, which means it is treated as acquisition debt and is not subject to the $1 million limit.

INTEREST DEDUCTION FOR RAW LAND?

Can I deduct interest on a loan for land that I plan to build a house on?

Interest on unimproved land is considered personal interest, which eventually will be phased out as a deduction. In 1987, 65 percent of the interest was deductible, 40 percent will be in 1988, 20 percent in 1989, 10 percent in 1990, and zero thereafter. Once you begin construction, 100 percent of mortgage interest is deductible.

POINTS

Are points deductible?

Yes they are. Points on a loan to buy your house can be 100 percent deductible in the year the loan is issued. However, the points cannot be borrowed as part of the loan amount and have to be paid separately. If the points are added to the loan proceeds, then they must be amortized over the life of the loan.

Points on a second mortgage or refinancing must be amortized over the term of the loan. When the house is sold, the remaining points are deductible. There is an exception: Points on VA or FHA loans are not deductible.

RV AS A SECOND HOME

I'm considering buying a recreational vehicle. Can I claim the motor home as a second home and deduct 100 percent of the interest from my taxes?

Yes, you can if you don't own another vacation home and the vehicle has a kitchen, bathroom, and bedroom. The deduction is also good for houseboats or anything the IRS will consider as a second vacation home. This is one of the few surviving deductions that were not eradicated by tax reform.

PRINCIPAL RESIDENCE

Does a recreational vehicle (mobile home or RV) or a boat qualify as a principal residence?

A principal residence is the place where you spend most of your time. A boat or an RV qualifies as long as it has a kitchen, bathroom, and sleeping accommodations.

CLOSING COSTS

I purchased my first house in 1987. The following closing costs were charged: points, appraisal, inspection, title report, and credit report. What can I deduct from my federal income taxes?

Points are deductible in full the year they are paid, if paid out of your private funds (not included in the loan proceeds). If the points are added into the loan proceeds, then the points are amortized over the life of the loan. The other closing costs are not deductible. However, the nondeductible closing costs can be added to the cost basis of your house. This will reduce the taxable profit incurred when you sell.

A special note about points and refinancing: When refinancing a home, points are always deducted over the life of the mortgage, no matter how they are paid.

RENTAL DEDUCTIONS

I understand there are now limits on the deduction for payment of interest. I own four houses, of which two are rentals. Explain to me how interest deductions differ and what the limits are.

After 1988, the deduction for the payment of interest is limited to $1 million on your two nonrental homes. The cost of interest on the other rentals is an expense deducted from rental income. But this also has certain limits that depend on your adjusted gross income (AGI) and when you bought the rentals. If your rental income minus rental expenses produced a net loss, you can deduct up to $25,000 from your salary income if your AGI was below $100,000. That deduction is reduced by 50 percent between $100,000 and $150,000 in AGI. Above $150,000 AGI losses are suspended, but you can use them to offset future rental income.

There is one exception: If you purchased the rentals before October 23, 1986, you can deduct 40 percent of your disallowed losses in 1988 whatever your income.

SELLING YOUR HOME

When I sell my home, do I have to pay taxes on the gain?

You can defer taxes on the gain as long as you buy within two years another home that's the same price or more than the home you sold. Additionally, if you are 55 or older, you have a once-in-a-lifetime, tax-free exemption on the first $125,000 in gain from the sale of your home. To qualify, you must have owned and lived in the home for at least three of the five years preceding the sale.

SELL YOUR HOME AND BUY A LESS EXPENSIVE HOME

In the event I sell my house and purchase a less expensive house, am I required to pay any taxes?

Yes, you are required to pay taxes on the difference between the cost of the new residence and the adjusted sales price of the old home. The adjusted sales price of your old home equals the selling price of your old home less its cost basis and all costs to sell it. The cost basis is determined by adding to the price of the home all the costs you incurred in purchasing it plus the cost of improvements.

TIME-SHARE DEDUCTIONS

Besides my home, I own two time-share condominiums which I'm entitled to use one week each. How much of the interest is deductible on all three properties?

You can deduct 100 percent of the interest on the loans used to buy your principal residence and one of the time-shares (considered a second home). Interest paid on the other time-share is considered personal interest, which is gradually being phased out. Personal interest is 40 percent deductible in 1988, 20 percent in 1989, 10 percent in 1990, and zero thereafter. The condo used for the second home must meet certain requirements. First, it must be used as security for the loan. Second, you actually have to own the property, even if for only one week of the year. Also, the way you take title to a time-share has a bearing on the qualification process. A "deeded" timeshare qualifies; however, a "right-to-use" agreement does not.

DEPRECIATING MOBILE HOMES

Recently I moved out of my mobile home and have since begun renting it out. Can I depreciate it over 27.5 years as I could for a rental house?

Yes, you can. Mobile homes under the new tax law are considered real property and can be depreciated over 27.5 years if a rental property. The old tax laws considered mobile homes as personal property and allowed depreciation over 5- or 10-year periods.

DEDUCTIBLE TAXES

What taxes are deductible?

You can deduct state and local income taxes, personal property taxes, and real estate taxes. Sales taxes are not deductible.

LOSS OF MONEY ON SALE OF RESIDENCE

I sold my house for less than was paid for it. Is the loss deductible?

Unfortunately, no. If you sell your principal residence for less than you paid for it, consider it lost money; it's not tax deductible.

MORTGAGE INTEREST TAX FORMS

I recently purchased my first home and in doing so have incurred a 30-year mortgage. Do I have to fill out a special form regarding the mortgage interest paid?

No. The form you're talking about (Form 8598) is required for those homeowners who took out home equity loans or second mortgages after August 16, 1986. The mortgage interest on your principal residence is an itemized deduction and goes on Schedule A.

RENTAL UNIT TAX ADVANTAGES

My mother earns $32,000 annually and wants to purchase a four-plex. If she lives in one unit and manages the others as rentals, what tax benefits would she receive?

Since your mother plans to reside in one of the units, she can deduct one-quarter of the mortgage interest and real estate taxes. On the remaining three-fourths she can take a business deduction for interest and taxes. She can also depreciate the rental portion over 27.5 years and deduct the costs of maintenance and utilities. Because she plans to manage the building actively, she can deduct up to $25,000 in losses from the building from regular salary income if the losses exceed any gains from other passive investments.

24 FORMS SECTION

The forms in this section are for your use as you see fit; permission is given for duplication of any of these forms.

APPLICATION TO RENT

Investment in real estate is essentially a money-making enterprise, not a charity. You have a lot invested, both in effort and money, so why in the world would you rent to a nonpaying deadbeat or a malicious tenant? Yet, time after time, inexperienced property owners rent out their beloved properties without taking the time to qualify prospective tenants. Remember, you are essentially lending your property to someone for a considerable period of time. A business relationship is about to develop and if you rent to someone who habitually pays late and isn't capable of taking reasonably good care of your property, you're in for plenty of trouble.

You can overcome most of the problems frequently encountered by novice landlords by properly qualifying your prospective renters. Good-paying tenants who will take good care of your property are a valuable asset. Here is some sound advice to assist you in judging whether or not your prospective tenants have the good character and capability of meeting the terms of your rental agreement.

After your prospect has completed filling out the rental application (see Figure 24.1), review it carefully. Make sure everything is legible and complete. Make sure the name is correct, because later on if Jim Jones skips the premises, he will be easier to trace with his complete name of James Anthony Jones. If more than one person will occupy the premises, get names of all the adults and find out who is responsible for rent payments.

Employment information is also very important. You definitely want to qualify the prospect on ability to pay rent. The rule of thumb is a range of 28 to 33 percent of gross monthly income can be safely

Home Work

Name ____________ Phone ____________ Phone ____________
Spouse/Roomate Name ____________ Work Ph. ____________
Unit to be occupied by ____________ Adults and ____ Children and ____ Pets
Present Address ____________ City ____________ State ____ Zip ____
Current Landlord/Mgr's Name ____________ Phone ____________
Why are you leaving? ____________
Previous Address ____________ City ____________ State ____ Zip ____
Landlord/Mgr's Name ____________ Phone ____________
Applicant's Birth Date ____________ Soc. Sec. # ______ Driv. Lic. ______
Applicant's Employer____________ Position ______ How long ______
Applicant's Employer's Address ____________ Gross monthly pay ______
Spouse/Roomate's Employer ____________ Gross monthly pay ______

Credit References: Bank ____________ Account # ______ Type ______
Other Active Reference ____________ Account # ______
Spouse/Roomate Credit Ref. ____________ Account # ______
In an emergency contact: ____________ Phone ____________
Address ____________ City ____________ State ____ Zip ____

List all motor vehicles, including RV's, to be kept at the dwelling unit. Include make, model, year, and license plate # for each.
Vehicle #1 ____________ Vehicle #2 ____________
License ____________ License ____________
Vehicle #3 ____________
License ____________

I (we) declare that the above information is correct and I (we) give my (our) permission for any reporting agency to release my credit file to undersigned landlord solely for the purposes of entering into a rental agreement. I (we) further authorize the Landlord or his agent to verify the above information including but not limited to contacting creditors, both listed herein or not, and present or former landlords.

Dated ____________, 19 ____ Applicant ____________

Applicant ____________

Figure 24.1. Application to rent

paid in rent. Lenders use a similar formula when making loans. If there are other debt obligations, such as credit cards, car payments and so on, then only a maximum of 28 percent should be applied toward rent; if there are none, then 33 percent of gross monthly income could be applied to rent payments. If your prospect qualifies by salary, then at an appropriate time you should verify employment. A simple phone call to the employer is sufficient.

Credit References

This information is supplied to a local credit bureau if it is necessary. What I usually do is, after the prospect has completed the rental application, I ask to see credit cards. If, in fact, the cards are active and up-to-date that satisfies any doubts I may have about credit worthiness. Just the fact that the prospect has Visa, MasterCard, or Sears credit cards is usually a good indication of credit-worthiness. One final credit check would be to call either the last or second-from-last landlord and inquire as to character and rent-paying habits.

Spouse/Roommate

You will have added protection by having the spouse or roommate sign all the documents of the rental agreement. This way both parties are jointly responsible, and it may be easier to locate one of the tenants if the other skips.

Discrimination Laws

As a landlord you cannot, by law, refuse to rent to people because of their race, creed, color, national origin, sex, or marital status. This doesn't mean, however, that you are obligated to rent to anyone just because they have the money. In particular for a multi-unit building, you should have certain standards to promote harmony in your building. For example, single adults prefer living in a building where other singles live. Families with children usually prefer to live in complexes that cater to other families. Similarly, senior citizens prefer to live where they're not annoyed by barking dogs and children at play. Therefore, set certain standards if you own multi-unit buildings and don't try and mix the elderly with the young or singles with families.

INVENTORY OF FURNISHINGS

This form (Figure 24.2) should accompany the lease for each unit. It identifies items such as the refrigerator, stove, couch, and so on, describes its current condition, and is useful later if there is a dispute about damages to be deducted from the security/cleaning deposits. The tenants may counter that the damage was there prior to moving in and, except in cases of gross and negligent damage, a defense of "the

Rental unit address ______________________________
Tenant ______________________ Inventory date ____________, 19 ______
____

Room	Item	Comments	Condition at Move-out

Tenant agrees that the above information is an accurate inventory and description and assumes responsibility for these items in the dwelling unit as of ____________________, 19 ____.

Move-in	Move-out
____________________ Date ________	____________________ Date ________
____________________ Date ________	____________________ Date ________

Figure 24.2. Inventory of furnishings

damage was there before we moved in" is difficult to overcome unless proper documentation is provided.

At the time of moving in, have the tenants go through the unit room by room with you. Have the tenants fill out the inventory and mark any comments and return the form to you. If comments cannot be made in the space provided, have your tenants make any additional comments on the reverse side of this form and note "See reverse side."

Address: ______________________ ________ KEY SIGNATURE ______________________

Orig. Move-In Date ____________

Lease Dated __________ Exp. ______

Tenant Tel. No. ____________

Date Due	Date Paid	Receipt Number	Paid To Noon	Amount Paid	Security Deposit	Cleaning Fee	Key Deposit #	Base Rent	Refrig-erator	Furniture	Parking	Month to Month	Additional Occupancy	Other Fireplace & Dishwasher	Air Conditioner	Utilities		Total Rent	Balance Due
DEPOSIT																			
RENT																			

BLDG. # ______ APT. ______ TYPE ______ FL. PL. ______ CLR. ______ NAME ______________________ Date Due ________

Figure 24.3. Cardex

CARDEX

A tenant record, or cardex, is a 5.5-by-8-inch card used by the owner or manager. It is a ready reference of all monies paid and due, plus other important tenant information, since every payment is recorded on the cardex. A sample cardex is shown in Figure 24.3.

NOTICE OF CHANGE IN TERMS OF RENTAL AGREEMENT

This form (Figure 24.4) is used to change the rental rate. Usually 30 days are required for a suitable notice before increasing the rental rate. Specific rental rates are found in the initial rental agreement. However, once the original term of the agreement expires, the landlord has the option to increase the rental rate.

REMINDERS TO PAY RENT

Delinquency by your tenants should not be tolerated. Good landlords should predictably react immediately to nonpayment of rent when it is due. Slow-paying tenants usually will react to this predictability and make the rent a high priority on their list of payments. Normally there is a three-day grace period after the rent due date. If the rent is not received within three days of due date, action has to be taken.

NOTICE OF CHANGE IN TERMS OF RENTAL AGREEMENT

Date ______________

To ______________________________, Tenant in possession of __________
____.

[ ] Certified mail
[ ] Hand delivered
[ ] Regular mail

You are hereby notified that the terms of tenancy under which you occupy the above address are to be changed as follows:

Effective ______________________, 19 ______, your rent will be increased by $ ______________ per month for a total of $ ____________ each month.

____
Landlord/Agent

Figure 24.4. Notice of change in terms of rental agreement

Collection experts agree that a first notice be sent within five days of the due date and a second notice after seven days. In the event your slow-paying tenant has a history of continued delinquency, a three-day notice to pay or quit the premises could be used rather than the second notice. Figures 24.5 and 24.6 are sample three-day and five-day reminders.

To ____________________________ Date ______________

____

Just a reminder that your rent was past due on ____________. According to the terms of your Rental Agreement, rent more than _______ days past due requires a late charge payment of $ __________. We would appreciate your prompt payment.

Thank you,

____

Landlord/Agent

Figure 24.5. Three-day reminder to pay rent

FIVE-DAY REMINDER TO PAY RENT

To ____________________________ Date ______________

____

Your rent is now past due as of ________________. As of this date, the past-due rent and late charges total $ _______________.

You must settle this account or our legal options will have to be considered. Therefore please act to remedy this matter immediately.

Thank you,

____

Landlord/Agent

Figure 24.6. Five-day reminder to pay rent

NOTICE TO PAY RENT OR QUIT THE PREMISES

This form (Figure 24.7) is the three-day pay or quit initiated by the landlord and issued to the tenant in default. Essentially, the tenant has three days from date of this notice to pay all monies in default or move out of the premises. This form is to be issued to the tenant only after the landlord has attempted to procure the amount owed through other means, such as the three- and five-day reminder notice. *Note:* Caution should be taken in this matter of the pay or quit notice because laws vary substantially on this matter throughout the country. This particular form may not conform to the laws in some states where new landlord/tenant statutes have been enacted. If this is the case, the landlord should seek the appropriate form at a reputable legal stationery store or consult with an attorney.

To ______________________________ Date ______________

____

[ ] Delivered by Marshal

[ ] Certified mail #______

[ ] Hand delivered

You are hereby notified that the rent for the period __________, 19 _____, to ______________, 19 _____, is now past due. As of this date, the total sum owing including late charges is $ _____________. Unless this sum is received within three days of this dated notice, you will be required to vacate and surrender the premises.

If it becomes necessary to proceed with legal action for the non-payment of rent or to obtain possession of the premises, as per the terms of the Rental Agreement, you will be liable for recovery of our reasonable attorney fees and expenses. You will also be liable for any additional rent for the time you are in possession of the premises.

____

Landlord/Agent

Figure 24.7. Notice to pay rent or quit the premises

NOTICE OF ABANDONED PROPERTY

Abandoned personal property that the tenant left behind for whatever reason has to be disposed of according to the prevailing laws within your particular state. If you carelessly dispose of abandoned property, whether it has value or not, you could leave yourself open to a legal suit by a malicious ex-tenant seeking revenge.

Abandoned-property statutes vary substantially from state to state. Junked or abandoned cars frequently are left behind also but are treated differently. If you should be faced with an old junker on your vacated property, it is best to call your local Department of Motor

Vehicles and find out the best way to dispose of it. Junk yards are usually not allowed to accept vehicles unless the car has a valid signed-off certificate of title.

Most states do require proof that an effort was in fact made to contact the rightful owner of the property. In most cases, this notice should be sufficient and should be sent to the rightful owner of the abandoned property at the last-known address. *Caution:* If there is obvious substantial value to the property in question or if you are not familiar with local statutes regarding this matter, consult with a qualified attorney.

Besides the notice of abandoned property form (Figure 24.8), I have also provided forms for financial statements (Figures 24.9 and 24.10) and an example of a residential lease (Figure 24.11).

To ______________________________ Date ______________
Address __________________________

When you vacated the rented unit located at ____________________ you left the following described property on the premises: ____.

You are hereby informed that unless you claim and remove the above-described property before __________________, 19_____, it will be thrown away, given to charity, or sold in a manner prescribed by law. If sold, the proceeds will be used to cover the cost of the sale, then to cover any sums due, and any remaining balance will be forwarded to you.

Please take care of this matter immediately.

____
Landlord/Agent

Figure 24.8. Notice of abandoned property

ASSETS:		
Cash on hand	______	
Cash in bank	______	
Car (vehicle)	______	
Life insurance (cash value)	______	
Real estate:	______	
Property "A"	______	
Property "B"	______	
Stocks and bonds	______	
Mortgages (owed to you)	______	
Accounts receivable	______	
Household furniture	______	
Other personal property	______	
TOTAL ASSETS:		______
LIABILITIES:		
Personal loans	______	
Vehicle	______	
Total real estate indebtedness	______	
Other (furniture, etc.)	______	
TOTAL LIABILITIES:		______
TOTAL NET WORTH:		______

Figure 24.9. Balance sheet

(MONTHLY INCOME AND EXPENSES)

MONTHLY INCOME:		
Gross wages	______	
Rental income	______	
Property "A"	______	
Property "B"	______	
Interest income	______	
Mortgage income	______	
Other income	______	
TOTAL MONTHLY INCOME:		______
MONTHLY EXPENSES:		
Rent	______	
Real estate loans	______	
Property "A"	______	
Property "B"	______	
Vehicle loan	______	
Furniture	______	
Personal loans	______	
Alimony or child support	______	
Other	______	
TOTAL MONTHLY EXPENSES:		______

Figure 24.10. Personal financial statement

1. This Lease made this ______________ day of ____________, 19 _____, by and between ____,
hereinafter called Landlord, and ____,
hereinafter called Tenant.

2. *Description*: Witnesseth, the Landlord, in consideration of the rents to be paid and the covenants and agreements to be performed by the Tenant, does hereby lease unto the Tenant the following described premises located thereon situated in the City of ________________________, County of ______________,
State of ____________________, commonly known as ______________________
____.

3. *Terms*: For the term of ________________________ (months/years) commencing on ______________________________, 19 ______, and ending on ______________
____, 19 ______.

4. *Rent*: Tenant shall pay Landlord, as rent for said premises, the sum of _______________ dollars ($ _____________) per month payable in advance on the first day of each month during the term hereof at Landlord's address above or said other place as Landlord may hereafter designate in writing. Tenant agrees to pay a $25 late fee if rent is not paid within five days of due date.

5. *Security Deposit*: Landlord herewith acknowledges the receipt of __________ ______________________________ dollars ($ _____________), which he is to retain as security for the faithful performance of the provisions of this Lease. If Tenant fails to pay rent, or defaults with respect to any provision of this Lease, Landlord may use the security deposit to cure the default or compensate Landlord for all damages sustained by Landlord. Tenant shall immediately on demand reimburse Landlord the sum equal to that portion of security deposit expended by Landlord so as to maintain the security deposit in the sum initially deposited with Landlord. If Tenant performs all obligations under this Lease, the security deposit, or that portion thereof that was not previously applied by Landlord, shall be returned to Tenant within 21 days after the expiration of this Lease, or after Tenant has vacated the premises.

6. *Possession*: It is understood that if the Tenant shall be unable to enter into and occupy the premises hereby leased at the time above provided, by reason of the said premises not being ready for occupancy, or by reason of holding over of any previous occupancy of said premises, the Landlord shall not be liable in damage to the Tenant therefore, but during the period the Tenant shall be unable to occupy said premises as hereinbefore provided, the rental therefore shall be abated and the Landlord is to be the sole judge as to when the premises are ready for occupancy.

7. *Use*: Tenant agrees that said premises during the term of this Lease shall be used and occupied by _______ adults and ______ children, and ______ animals, and for no purpose whatsoever other than a residence, without the written consent of the Landlord, and that Tenant will not use the premises for any

Figure 24.11. Rental agreement residential lease

purpose in violation of any law, municipal ordinance, or regulation, and at any breach of this agreement the Landlord may at his option terminate this Lease and re-enter and repossess the leased premises.

8. *Utilities*: Tenant will pay for all charges for all water supplied to the premises and pay for all gas, heat, electricity, and other services supplied to the premises, except as herein provided: ______________________________.

9. *Repairs and Maintenance*: The Landlord shall at his expense, except for the first $100 in cost which the Tenant pays, keep and maintain the exterior walls, roof, electrical wiring, heating and air-conditioning system, water heater, built-in appliances, and water lines in good condition and repair, except where damage has been caused by negligence or abuse of the Tenant, in which case Tenant shall repair same at his sole expense.

Tenant hereby agrees that the premises are now in good condition and shall at his sole expense maintain the premises and appurtenances in the manner in which they were received, reasonable wear and tear excepted.

The ______________________________ agrees to maintian landscaping and swimming pool (if any). Tenant agrees to adequately water landscaping.

10. *Alterations and Additions*: The Tenant shall not make any alterations, additions, or improvements to said premises without the Landlord's written consent. All alterations, additions, or improvements made by either of the parties hereto upon the premises, except movable furniture, shall be the property of the Landlord and shall remain upon and be surrendered with the premises at the termination of this Lease.

11. *Assignment*: The Tenant will not assign or transfer this lease or sublet said premises without the written consent of the Landlord.

12. *Default*: If the Tenant shall abandon or vacate said premises before the end of the term of this lease, or if default shall be made by the tenant in the payment of said rent or any part hereof, or if the Tenant shall fail to perform any of the Tenant's agreements in this lease, then and in each and every instance of such abandonment or default, the Tenant's right to enter said premises shall be suspended, and the Landlord may at his option enter said premises and remove and exclude the Tenant from said premises.

13. *Entry by Landlord*: Tenant shall allow the Landlord or his agents to enter the premises at all reasonable times and upon reasonable notice for the purpose of inspecting or maintaining the premises or to show it to prospective tenants or purchasers.

14. *Attorney's fees*: The Tenant agrees to pay all costs, expenses, and reasonable attorney's fees including obtaining advice of counsel incurred by Landlord in enforcing by legal action or otherwise any of Landlord's rights under this lease or under any law of this state.

15. *Holding Over*: If Tenant, with the Landlord's consent, remains in possession of the premises after expiration of the term of this lease, such possession will be deemed a month-to-month tenancy at a rental equal to the last monthly

Figure 24.11. Rental agreement residential lease (continued)

rental, and upon all the provisions of this lease applicable to such a month-to-month tenancy.

The parties hereto have executed this Lease on the date first above written.

Landlord	Tenant
By: ______________________	By: ______________________
	By: ______________________

Figure 24.11. Rental agreement residential lease (continued)

GLOSSARY OF REAL ESTATE DEFINITIONS

Abandonment The voluntary relinquishment of rights of ownership or another form of interest (an easement) by failure to use the property over an extended period of time.

Absentee landlord A lessor of real property (usually the owner) who does not reside on any portion of the property.

Abstract of title A summary of the conveyances, transfers, and any other data relied on as evidence of title, together with any other elements of record which may impair the title. Still in use,in some states, but giving way to the use of title insurance.

Accelerated depreciation Depreciation occurring at a rate faster than the normal rate. This form of depreciation is usually used for special assets for income tax purposes.

Acceleration clause A clause in a mortgage or trust deed giving the lender the right to call all monies owed to be immediately due and payable upon the happening of a certain stated event.

Acceptance Refers to a legal term denoting acceptance of an offer. A buyer offers to buy and the seller accepts the offer.

Access right A right to enter and exit one's property.

Accretion Gradual deposit of soil from a waterway onto the adjoining land. The additional land generally becomes the property of the owner of the shore or bank, except where local statutes specify otherwise.

Accrued depreciation The amount of depreciation accumulated over a period of time in the accounting system for replacement of an asset.

Acknowledgment A formal declaration of execution of a document before an authorized official (usually a notary public) by a person who has executed (signed) a document.

Acre A measure of land, equal to 160 sq. rods (43,560 sq. ft.). An acre is approximately 209 × 209 feet.

Addendum Something added. A list or other items added to a document. letter, contract, escrow instructions, etc.

Adjustable-rate mortgage (ARM) Mortgage with an interest rate that can change as often as specified.

Adjusted-cost basis The value of an asset on the accounting books of a taxpayer that is the original cost plus improvements less depreciation.

Adjusted sales price Equals, for income tax purposes, the selling price of your house less its acquisition cost and all the costs to sell it.

Adverse land use A use of land that causes the surrounding property to lose value, such as a truck terminal adjacent to a residential area.

Adverse possession A method of acquiring title by open and notorious possession under an evident claim or right. Specific requirements for time of possession usually vary with each state.

Affidavit A written statement or declaration sworn to or affirmed before some official who has the authority to administer affirmation. An oath.

Agency agreement (listing) A listing agreement between the seller of real property and a broker wherein the broker's commission is protected against a sale by other agents but not by the principal (seller). Often referred to as a nonexclusive agency listing.

Agent A person authorized to represent or act for another in business matters.

Agreement of sale A written contract between the buyer and the seller, where both parties are in full agreement on the terms and conditions of the sale.

Alienation The transfer of property from one person to another.

Alienation clause A clause within a loan instrument calling for a debt to be paid in its entirety upon the transfer of ownership of the secured property. Similar to a "due-on-sale" clause.

All-Inclusive Trust Deed (AITD) Same as wrap-around mortgage except a deed of trust is the security instrument instead of a mortgage.

Alluvion Soil deposited by accretion.

Amenities Attractive or desirable features of a property, such as a swimming pool or view of the ocean.

American Land Title Association (ALTA) A group of title insurance companies that issues title insurance to lenders.

Amortization The liquidation of a financial obligation using regular equal payments on an installment basis.

Annuity (1) Cash payment over a given period. (2) A fixed amount given or left by will paid periodically.

Appraisal An estimate and opinion of value: an objective conclusion resulting from an analysis of pertinent data.

Appreciation Increase in value of property from improvements or the elimination of negative factors.

Appurtenance Something belonging to the land and conveyed with it, such as buildings, fixtures, and rights.

ARM See adjustable-rate mortgage.

ASHI American Society of Home Inspectors.

Assemblage Process of acquiring contiguous properties into one overall parcel for a specific use or to increase value of the whole.

Assessed value Value placed on property by the tax assessor.

Assessment The valuation of property for the purpose of levying a tax, or the amount of the tax levied.

Assessor One appointed to assess property for taxation.

Assigned mortgage A note which is transferred to another. For example, a note owed to you is an asset that someone is paying you interest on that can be assigned to another.

Assignee One who receives an assignment. (Assignor: one who owns property assigned.)

Assignment A transfer or making over to another the whole of any property, real or personal, or of any estate or right therein. To assign is to transfer.

Assumption of mortgage The agreement of a buyer to assume the liability of an existing mortgage. Normally, the lender has to approve the new borrower before the existing borrower is released from the liability.

Attachment Seizure of property by court order, usually done in a pending law suit to make property available in case of judgment.

Balance sheet A financial statement that shows the true condition of a business or individual as of a particular date. Discloses assets, liabilities, and net worth.

Balloon payment The final installment paid at the end of the term of a note; used only when preceding installments were not sufficient to pay off the note in full.

Bankruptcy Procedure of federal law to seize the property of a debtor and divide the proceeds among the creditors.

Base and meridian Imaginary lines used by surveyors to find and describe the location of public or private lands.

Benchmark A mark used by surveyors that is permanently fixed in the ground to denote height of that point in relation to sea level.

Beneficiary The lender involved in a note and trust deed. One entitled to the benefit of a trust.

Bequeath To give or leave personal property by a will.

Bill of sale An instrument used to transfer personal property.

Blanket mortgage (trust deed) A single mortgage, or trust deed, that covers more than one piece of real estate.

Blighted area A declining area where property values are affected by destructive economic or natural forces.

Block busting A method of informing a community of the fact that people of a different race or religion are moving into the neighborhood; this often causes property values to drop, thereby enabling homes to be obtained at below market value.

Boardfoot A unit of measuring lumber. One boardfoot is 12 by 12 by 1 inch, or 144 cubic inches.

Bond An insurance agreement by which one party is insured against loss or default by another. In the construction business a performance bond ensures the interested party that the contractor will complete the project. A bond can also be a method of financing debt by a government or corporation; the bond is interest-bearing and has priority over stock in terms of security.

Book value The value of an asset plus improvements less depreciation.

Boot A term used when trading property. "Boot" is the additional value given when trading properties in order to equalize values.

Bottom land Low-lying ground such as a valley. Also low land along a waterway formed by alluvial deposits.

Breach Violation of an obligation in a contract.

British Thermal Unit (BTU) Describes the capacity of heating and cooling systems. It is the unit of heat required to raise one pound of water one degree Fahrenheit.

Broker (real estate) An agent licensed by the state to carry on the business of dealing in real estate. He or she usually receives a commission for services of bringing together buyers and sellers, or tenants and landlords.

Building code A set of laws that control the design, materials, and similar factors in the construction of buildings.

Building line A line set by law or deed restricting a certain distance from the street line, in front of which an owner cannot build on a lot. Also known as a setback line.

Built-ins Items that are not movable, such as stoves, ovens, microwave ovens, and dishwashers.

Built-up roof A form of level roof consisting of layers of roofing materials covered with fine gravel.

Business opportunity The sale or lease of a business and good will of an existing business enterprise.

Buyers' market A market condition in real estate in which more homes are for sale than there are interested buyers.

Capital expenditures Money spent by a business on improvements such as land, building, and machinery.

Capital gains A term used for income tax purposes; it represents the gain realized from the sale of an asset less the purchase price and deductible expenses. (Before the 1986 tax reform, capital gains rules allowed 60 percent exclusion from taxes on the sale of an asset if it was a capital gain.)

Capitalization An appraising term used in determining value by considering net-operating income and a percentage of reasonable return on investment.

Capitalization rate A percentage used by an investor to determine the value of income property through capitalization.

Cash flow The owner's spendable income after operating expenses and debt service are deducted.

Caveat emptor A legal phrase meaning "let the buyer beware." The buyer takes the risk when purchasing an item without the protection of warranties.

Certificate of Reasonable Value (CRV) An appraisal of real property issued by the Veteran's Administration.

Chain of title A history of conveyances and encumbrances affecting the title to real property as far back as records are available.

Chattel Personal property.

Chattel mortgage A mortgage on personal property, as distinguished from one on real property.

Client One who employs another's services, such as an attorney, real estate agent, insurance agent.

Closing In the sale of real estate the final moment when all documents are executed and recorded and the sale is complete. Also a general selling term where a salesperson is attempting to sell something and the buyer agrees to purchase.

Closing costs Incidental expenses incurred with the sale of real property, such as appraisal fees, title insurance, termite report, and so on.

Closing statement A list of the final accounting of all monies of both buyer and seller and prepared by an escrow agent. It notes all costs each must pay at the completion of a real estate transaction.

Cloud on title An encumbrance on real property that affects the rights of the owner, which often keeps the title from being marketable until the "cloud" is removed.

Collateral security A separate obligation attached to another contract pledging something of value to guarantee performance of the contract.

Commercial bank An institution for checking accounts, loans, savings accounts, and other services usually not found in savings and loan associations. Banks are active in installment loans on vehicles, boats, and construction financing rather than on long-term real estate financing. See also Institutional Lenders.

Common area That area owned in common by owners of condominiums and planned unit-development homes within a subdivision.

Community property Both real and personal property accumulated by a husband and wife after marriage.

Compound interest Interest paid on the original principal and on interest accrued.

Condemnation A declaration by governing powers that a structure is unfit for use.

Conditional sales contract A contract for the sale of property where the buyer has possession and use, but the seller retains title until the conditions of the contract have been fulfilled. Also known as a land contract.

Condominium A system of individual ownership of units in a multi-unit structure where each space is individually owned but each owner jointly owns the common areas and land.

Conformity, principle of An appraising term stating that uniformity throughout a certain area produces highest value.

Conservator A court-appointed guardian.

Consideration Anything of value given to induce someone into entering into a contract.

Construction loan The short-term financing of improvements on real estate. Once the improvements are completed, a "take-out" loan for a longer term is used to pay off the existing construction loan.

Contingency A condition upon which a valid contract is dependent. For example, the sale of a house is contingent upon the buyer's obtaining adequate financing.

Contract An agreement between two or more parties, written or oral, to do or not to do certain things.

Contract of sale Same as Conditional Sales Contract or a Land Contract.

Conventional loan A loan made, usually on real estate, that is not backed by the federal agencies of FHA and VA.

Convertible ARM Adjustable-rate mortgage which can convert to a fixed-rate mortgage.

Conveyance The transfer of the title to land from one party to another.

Cooperative apartment A building with two or more units in which the unit owners are required to purchase stock in the corporation that owns the property. The coop was a forerunner to the condominium and is not as popular because of the difficulty in financing, since there is no individual ownership of each unit.

Corporation A legal entity having certain powers and duties of a natural person, together with rights and liabilities of both, distinct and apart from those persons composing it.

Cost approach A method of appraisal whereby the estimated cost of a structure is calculated, less the land value and depreciation.

Counteroffer An offer in response to an offer. A offers to buy B's house for $80,000 although it is listed for $85,000. B counteroffers A by stating that she will sell the house to A for $81,000. The $81,000 is a counteroffer.

Covenants Agreements written into deeds and other instruments stating performance or nonperformance of certain acts or noting certain uses or nonuses of the property.

CPM Certified Property Manager.

Cul de sac A dead-end street with a turn-around included.

Current assets An accounting term representing assets that can readily be converted into cash, as with short-term accounts receivable and common stocks.

Current liabilities Short-term debts.

D.B.A. (Doing Business As) A business name or identification.

Dedication The donation by an owner of private property for public use.

Deed A written instrument that when executed conveys title of real property.

Default Failure to fulfill or discharge an obligation or to perform any act that has been agreed to in writing.

Defendant The individual or entity against whom a civil or criminal action is brought.

Deferred payments Payments to begin in the future.

Deflation Opposite of inflation. The price of goods and services decrease in relation to the money available to buy them.

Delivery The placing of property in the possession of the grantee.

Demise A transfer of an estate by lease or will.

Demographics Statistics. Data used by certain businesses (especially chain stores) such as the traffic court regarding a possible new location.

Density The amount of crowding together of buildings, people, or other given things.

Depletion The reduction or loss in value of an asset.

Deposit receipt The form used to accept the earnest-money deposit to secure the offer for the purchase of real property.

Depreciation Loss of value of an asset brought about by age (positive deterioration) or functional and economic obsolescence. Percentage reduction of property value year by year for tax purposes.

Depression That part of a business cycle where unemployment is high and production and overall purchasing by the public is low. A severe recession.

Deterioration The gradual wearing away of a building from exposure to the elements. Also referred to as physical depreciation.

Devise A gift of real estate by will.

Diluvium A deposit of land left by a flood.

Diminishing returns An economic theory stating that an increase in capital or manpower will not increase production proportionately (four laborers may do less than four times the work of one laborer; and two laborers may do more than twice the work of one laborer). The return diminishes when production is proportionately less than input.

Directional growth The path of development of an urban area. Used to determine where future development will be most profitable.

Divided interest Different interest in the same property, as in interest of the owner, lessee, or mortgagee.

Documentary tax stamps Stamps affixed to a deed denoting the amount of transfer tax paid.

Domicile The place where a person has a permanent home.

Double-declining depreciation An accelerated method of depreciating an asset in which double the amount of straignt-line depreciation is used.

Dower The portion of her husband's estate that a wife inherits on his death.

Down payment Cash or other consideration paid toward a purchase by the buyer, as opposed to that amount which is financed.

Due-on-sale clause A condition written into a financial instrument which gives the lender the right to require immediate repayment of the unpaid balance if the property is sold without consent of the lender.

Easement The legal right-of-way that permits an owner to cross another's land so as to get to his or her own property. Easement is appurtenant to the land and thus cannot be sold off separately and must be transferred with the title to the land of which it is part. Other forms of rights and privileges with respect to adjacent or nearby land can be created by agreement and are also called easements to the property.

Economic life The period over which property will yield a return on the investment.

Economic obsolescence Loss of useful life and desirability of a property through economic forces, such as change in zoning, changes in traffic flow, and so on, rather than deterioration.

Economic rent The current market rental based on comparable rent for a similar unit.

Effective age The age of a structure estimated by its condition as opposed to its actual age.

Egress The right to go out across the land of another.

Elevation The height above sea level. Architecturally, the view looking at the front of a structure.

Emblements Crops growing on the land.

Eminent domain The right of the government to acquire private property for public use by condemnation. The owner must be fully compensated.

Encroachment Trespass. The building or any improvements partly or wholly on the property of another.

Encumbrance Anything that affects or limits the fee simple title to property, such as mortgages, trust deeds, easements, or restrictions of any kind. Liens are special encumbrances that make the property security for the debt.

Entity An existence or being, as in a corporation or business, rather than an individual.

Entrepreneur An independent businessperson taking risks for profit, as opposed to a salaried employee working for someone else.

Equity The value that an owner has in property over and above the liens against it. A legal term based on fairness rather than strict interpretation of the law.

Equity build-up The reduction in the difference between property value and the amount of the lien as regular payments are made. The equity increases (builds up) on an amortized loan as the proportion of interest payment gets smaller, causing the amount going toward principal to increase.

Equity participation See equity sharing.

Equity partnership See equity sharing.

Equity sharing Shared ownership of real property. Also known as shared equity, equity participation, equity partnership, and shared appreciation.

Escalation clause A clause in a lease providing for an increase in rent at a future time because of increased costs to lessor, as in cost-of-living index, tax increases, and so on.

Escheat The reverting of property to the state in the absence of heirs.

Escrow A neutral third party who carries out the provisions of an agreement between two or more parties.

Estate The ownership interest of a person in real property. Often used to describe a large home with spacious grounds. Also a deceased person's property.

Estate for years Any estate for a specific period of time. A lease.

Exclusive right-to-sell listing A written contract between agent and owner in which the agent has the right to collect a commission if the listed property is sold by anyone during the terms of agreement.

Executor The person appointed in a will to carry out the terms of the will.

Face value The value stated on the face of notes, mortgages, and so on, without consideration of any discounting.

Fair market value The price a property will bring given that both buyer and seller are fully aware of market conditions and comparable properties.

Feasibility survey A study of an area prior to development of a project in order to determine whether the project will be successful.

FED See Federal System Reserve System.

Federal Deposit Insurance Corporation (FDIC) The federal corporation that insures bank depositors against loss up to a specified amount, currently $100,000.

Federal Home Loan Bank Board The board that charters and regulates Federal Savings and Loan Associations and Federal Home Loan Banks.

Federal Home Loan Banks Regulated by the Federal Home Loan Bank Board. Currently 11 regional branches where banks, savings and loans, insurance companies, or similar institutions may join the system and borrow for the purpose of making available home-financing money. Its purpose is to make a permanent supply of financing available for home loans.

Federal Home Loan Mortgage Corporation (FHLMC) (Freddie Mac) A federal agency that purchases first mortgages from members of the Federal Reserve System and the Federal Home Loan Bank system.

Federal Housing Administration (FHA) The federal agency that insures first mortgages on homes (and other projects), enabling lenders to extend more lenient terms to borrowers.

Federal National Mortgage Association (FNMA) (Fannie Mae) A private corporation that purchases first mortgages at discounts.

Federal Reserve System Commonly referred to as the "Fed," which consists of a twelve member Federal Open Market Committee, twelve Fed branches, plus approximately 6,000 member banks. Its primary purpose is to control the supply of money.

Federal Savings and Loan Insurance Corporation (FSLIC) A federal corporation that insures deposits in savings and loan associations up to a specified amount, currently $125,000.

Fee simple Ownership of title to property without any limitation, which can be sold, left at will, or inherited.

Fiduciary A person in a position of trust and confidence, as between principal and broker; broker as fiduciary owes loyalty to the principal, which cannot be breached under rules of agency.

First mortgage A mortgage having priority over all other voluntary liens against a specific property.

Fixed-rate mortgage A mortgage loan wherein the rate of interest charged the borrower remains constant over its term.

Fixtures Items, such as plumbing, electrical fixtures, etc., affixed to buildings or land usually in such a way that they cannot be removed without damage to themselves or the property.

Foreclosure Procedure in which property pledged for security for a debt is sold at public auction to pay the debt in the event of default in payment and terms.

Free and clear A specific property has no liens, especially voluntary liens, against it.

Front footage The linear measurement along the front of a parcel. That portion of the parcel that fronts the street or walkway.

Functional obsolescence Loss in value of out-of-date or poorly designed equipment while newer equipment and structures have been invented since its construction.

Government National Mortgage Association (GNMA) (Ginnie Mae) Purchases first mortgages at discounts, similar to that of FNMA.

Graduated lease A lease that provides for rental adjustments, often based upon future determination of the cost-of-living index. Used for the most part in long-term leases.

Graduated payment mortgage (GPM) Increases in payment over its term.

Grant A transfer of interest in real property, such as an easement.

Grantee One to whom the grant is made.

Grantor The one who grants the property or its rights.

Gross income Total scheduled income from property before any expenses are deducted.

Gross-income multiplier A general appraising rule of thumb that when multiplied by the gross annual income of a property will estimate the market value. For example, the property sells for 7.2 times the gross.

Gross lease A lease obligating the lessor to pay all or part of the expenses incurred on a leased property.

Ground lease A lease of vacant land.

Ground rent Rent paid for vacant land.

Growing equity mortgage (GEM) Increases in payment over a specified term. Increases are applied directly to principal reduction.

Hardwood Wood, such as oak, maple, and walnut, used for interior finish, as opposed to certain other soft woods.

Highest and best use An appraisal term for the use of land that will bring the highest economic return over a given time.

Homeowners association An association of homeowners within a community formed to improve and maintain the quality of the community. An association formed by the developer of condominiums or planned-unit developments.

Homestead A declaration by the owner of a home that protects the home against judgments up to specified amounts provided by certain state laws.

Hypothecate To give a thing as security without giving up possession of it, as with mortgaging real property.

Impound account A trust account held for the purpose of paying taxes, insurance, and other periodic expenses incurred with real property.

Improvements A general term to describe buildings, roads, and utilities that have been added to raw (unimproved) land.

Inflation The increase in an economy over its true or natural growth. Usually identified with rapidly increasing prices.

Installment note A note that provides for regular monthly payments to be paid on the date specified in the instrument.

Institutional lenders Banks, savings and loans, or other businesses who make loans to the public during their ordinary course of business, as opposed to individuals who fund loans.

Instrument A written legal document.

Intangible value The good will or well-advertised name of an established business.

Interest (1) Money charged for the use of money (principal). (2) A share or right in some property.

Interim loan A short-term loan usually for real estate improvements during the period of construction.

Intestate A person who dies without having made a will.

Intrinsic value The value of a thing by itself without certain aspects which will add value to some and not to others, as with a vintage Rolls Royce, which might have value to a car collector, but to few others.

Investment The laying out of money in the purchase of some form of property intending to earn a profit.

Involuntary lien A lien that attaches to property without consent of the owner, such as tax liens as opposed to voluntary liens (mortgages).

Joint tenancy Joint ownership by two or more persons with right of survivorship. Upon the death of a joint tenant, the interest does not go to the heirs but to the remaining joint tenants.

Junior mortgage A mortgage lower in priority than a first mortgage, such as second and third mortgages.

Land contract A contract for the sale of property where the buyer has possession and use, but the seller retains title until certain conditions of the contract have been fulfilled. Same as a conditional sales contract.

Land grant A gift of public land by the federal government.

Landlord The owner of rented property.

Lease A contract between the owner of real property, called the lessor, and another person or party referred to as the lessee, covering the conditions by which the lessee may occupy and use the property.

Lease with option to purchase A lease under which the lessee has the option to purchase the leased property, the terms of which must be set forth in the lease.

Legacy A gift of personal property by will.

Legal description The geographical identification of a parcel of land.

Legatee One who receives personal property from a will.

Lessee One who contracts to rent property under a specified lease.

Lessor An owner who contracts into a lease with a tenant (lessee).

Leverage The use of a small amount of cash to control a much greater value of assets.

Liability A term covering all types of debts and obligations.

Lien An encumbrance against real property for money as in taxes, mortgages, and judgments.

Life estate An estate in real property for the life of a person.

Limited partnership A partnership of one or more general partners that operates a business along with one or more limited partners who contribute capital. This arrangement limits certain of the partners' liability to the amount of money contributed.

Liquidate Disposal of property or assets or the settlement of debts.

Lis pendens A recorded legal notice showing pending litigation of real property. Anyone acquiring an interest in such property after the recording of *lis pendens* could be bound to the outcome of the litigation.

Listing A contract between owner and broker to sell the owner's real property.

Loan-To-Value Ratio (LTVR) The ratio, expressed as a percentage, of the amount of a loan to the value of real property.

Long-term capital gain Prior to the 1986 tax reform it was a preferential tax treatment excluding 60 percent of the gain incurred on the sale of an asset held for at least six months.

MAI (Member Appraisal Institute) A designation issued to a member of the American Institute of Real Estate Appraisers after meeting specific qualifications.

Maintenance reserve Money held in reserve to cover anticipated maintenance expenses.

Margin For lending purposes, that amount added to a certain index rate which results in the rate of interest charged to the borrower.

Marketable title A saleable title free of objectionable liens or encumbrances.

Market-data approach An appraisal method to determine value by comparing similar properties to the subject property.

Market value The price a buyer will pay and a seller will accept, both being fully informed of market conditions.

Master plan A comprehensive zoning plan to allow a city to grow in an orderly manner.

Mechanics lien A lien created by statute on a specific property for labor or materials contributed to an improvement on that property.

Metes and Bounds A legal description used in describing boundary lines.

Mineral rights Ownership of the minerals beneath the ground. The owner of mineral rights doesn't necessarily own the surface land.

Moratorium Temporary suspension of the enforcement of liability for a debt.

Mortgage An instrument by which property is hypothecated to secure the payment of a debt.

Mortgage broker A person who, for a fee, brings together the lender with the borrower. Also known as a loan broker.

Mortgage Guaranty Insurance Corporation (MGIC) Private corporation that insures mortgage loans.

Mortgagee One who lends the money and receives the mortgage.

Mortgagor One who borrows on a property and gives a mortgage as security.

Multiple listing service (MLS) A listing taken by a member of an organization of brokers, whereby all members have an opportunity to find a buyer.

Net income Gross income less operating expenses.

Net lease A lease requiring tenant to pay all or part of the expenses on leased property in addition to the stipulated rent.

Net listing A listing whereby an agent may retain as compensation all sums received over and above a net price to the owner. Illegal in some states.

Net worth Total assets less liabilities of an individual, corporation, or business.

Nonexclusive listing A listing in which the agent has an exclusive listing with respect to other agents; however, the owner may sell the property without being liable for a commission.

Notary public One who is authorized by federal or local government to attest authentic signatures and administer oaths.

Note A written instrument acknowledging a debt and promising payment.

Notice to quit A notice issued by landlord to the tenant to vacate rented property, usually for nonpayment of rent or breach of contract.

Offer A presentation to form a contract or agreement.

Open listing An authorization given by an owner to a real estate agent to sell the owner's property. Open listings may be given to more than one agent without liability, and only the one who secures a buyer on satisfactory terms gets paid a commission.

Operating expenses Expenses relevant to income-producing property, such as taxes, management, utilities, insurance, and other day-to-day costs.

Option A right given, for consideration, to purchase or lease property upon stipulated terms within a specific period of time.

Passive activity New definition under the 1986 tax reform. A passive activity is any activity that involves the conduct of any trade or business in which you do not materially participate. Any rental activity will be a passive activity even if you materially participate. Prior to the tax reform, passive losses could offset other forms of income; subsequent to the act, the taxpayer is limited to this benefit.

Percentage lease A lease on property in which normally a minimum specified rent is paid or a percentage of gross receipts of the lessee is paid, whichever is higher.

Personal property Property that is not real property (real estate).

Planned development Five or more individually owned lots where one or more other parcels are owned in common or there are reciprocal rights in one or more other parcels; subdivision.

Plat book A book containing plat maps of a certain area.

Plat map A map or plan of a specified parcel of land.

Point One percent. A 1-point fee often charged by the lender to originate the loan. On FHA and VA loans, the seller pays points to accommodate the loan.

Power of attorney An instrument authorizing a person to act as the agent of the person granting the power.

Preliminary title report The report of condition of the title before a sale or loan transaction. Once completed, a title insurance policy is issued.

Prepayment penalty A penalty within a note, mortgage, or trust deed, imposing a penalty if the debt is paid in full before the end of its terms.

Prime lending rate The most favorable interest rate charged by an institutional lender to its best customers.

Principal The employer of an agent. Also, the amount of debt, not including interest.

Private Mortgage Insurance (PMI) Insurance on a portion of the first mortgage allowing the lender to offer more lenient terms to a borrower.

Proration of taxes To divide or prorate the taxes equally or proportionately to time of use.

Purchase agreement An agreement between buyer and seller denoting price and terms of the sale.

Purchase money mortgage A mortgage given by the buyer to the seller as part of the purchase consideration.

Pyramid To build an estate by multiple acquisitions of properties using the initial properties for a base for further investment.

Quitclaim deed A deed used to remove clouds on a title by relinquishing any right, title, or interest that the grantor may have.

Real Estate Investment Trust (REIT) A method of group investment with certain tax advantages. It is governed by federal and state laws.

Realtor A real estate broker holding membership in a real estate board affiliated with the National Association of Realtors.

Redemption The buying back of one's property after it has been lost through foreclosure. Payment of delinquent taxes after sale to the state.

Rent Consideration, usually money, for the occupancy and use of real property.

Replacement-cost method A method of appraisal to determine value by determining an exact replica.

Request for notice of default A request by a lender that is recorded for notification in the case of default by a loan with priority.

Reverse annuity mortgage (RAM) A mortgage in which the borrower is paid an annuity (income) drawn against the equity in the home.

Right of survivorship Right to acquire the interest of a deceased joint owner. Distinguishing characteristic of joint tenancy.

Right of way A privilege given by the owner of a property to given another the right to pass over private land.

Riparian rights The right of a landowner to water on, under, or adjacent to the land owned.

Sale-leaseback A sale of a subsequent lease from the buyer back to the seller.

Savings and Loan Association An institution that retains deposits for savers and lends out these deposits for home loans.

Secondary financing A junior loan or second in priority to a first mortgage or trust deed.

Security deposit Money given to a landlord by the tenant to secure performance of the rental agreement.

Sellers' market A time when there are more buyers than sellers.

Separate property Property owned by husband or wife that is not community property. Property acquired before marriage or by a gift, will, or inheritance.

Service point What the lender charges, in addition to interest, to originate the loan, one service point represents 1 percent of the loan amount.

Severalty An estate held by one person alone, an individual right. The term is misleading as it does not mean several persons own it. Distinguished from joint tenancy.

Shared appreciation See equity sharing.

Shared appreciation mortgage (SAM) A mortgage that allows the lender to share in the appreciation of the property in return for a lower rate of interest.

Sheriff's deed Deed given by court order in connection with the sale of a property to satisfy a judgment.

Single-family residence A general term to distinguish a house from an apartment house, a condominium, or a planned-unit development.

Society of Real Estate Appraisers (SRA) One is designated a Senior Residential Appraiser after receiving experience and education in the field of appraising.

Special assessment Legal charge against real estate by public authority to pay the cost of public improvements (for example, sewers) by which the property is benefited.

Speculator One who buys property with the intent of selling it quickly at a profit.

Straight-line depreciation Reducing value for tax purposes over an extended period of time by equal increments.

Straight note A nonamortized note promising to repay a loan, signed by the debtor and including the amount, date due, and interest rate.

Subdivision A division of one parcel of land into smaller lots.

Subject-to mortgage When a buyer takes title to real property "subject-to mortgage," buyer is not responsible to the holder of the note. The original maker of the note is not released from the liability of the note and the most the new buyer can lose in foreclosure is equity in the property.

Sublease A lease given by a lessee.

Syndicate A group of investors who invest in one or more properties through a partnership, corporation, or trust.

Take-out commitment Agreement by a lender to have available a long-term loan over a specified time once construction is completed.

Tax base The assessed value multipled by the tax rate to determine the amount of tax due.

Tax sale A sale of property, usually at auction, for nonpayment of taxes assessed against it.

Tenancy in common Ownership by two or more persons who hold an undivided interest without right of survivorship.

Tenant The holder of real property under a rental agreement. Also referred to as a lessee.

Tender An offer of money, usually in satisfaction of a claim or demand.

Tenements All rights in land which pass with the conveyance of the land. Also commonly refers to certain groups of multiple dwellings.

Testator A person who leaves a legally valid will at death.

Tight money A condition in the money market in which demand for the use of money exceeds the available supply.

Timeshare Shared ownership wherein the owners are allowed limited use of a property.

Title insurance Insurance written by a title company to protect the property owner against loss if title is imperfect.

Topography Character of the surface of land. Topography may be level, rolling or mountainous.

Township A territorial subdivision six miles long, six miles wide, and containing 36 sections, each one mile square.

Tract house A house similar to other homes within a subdivision and built by the same developer, as opposed to a custom home built to owner specifications.

Trade fixtures Personal property of a business that is attached to the property, but can be removed upon the sale of the property.

Trust deed An instrument that conveys legal title of a property to a trustee to be held pending fulfillment of an obligation, usually the repayment of a loan to a beneficiary (lender).

Trustee One who holds bare legal title to a property in trust for another to secure performance of a debt obligation.

Trustor The borrower of money secured by a trust deed.

Unimproved land Land in its natural state without structures on it.

Unlawful detainer An action of law to evict a person or persons illegally occupying real property.

Usury Interest rate charged on a loan in excess of that permitted by law.

Variable-interest rate A fluctuating interest rate that can go up or down depending on the market rate.

Vendee A purchaser or buyer.

Vendor A seller.

Vested Bestowed upon someone or secured by someone, such as title to property.

Voluntary lien A voluntary lien by the owner, such as a mortgage, as opposed to an involuntary lien (for example, taxes).

Waive To relinquish, or abandon. To forgo a right to enforce or require anything.

Wrap-around mortgage A second mortgage that is subordinate to but includes the face value of the first mortgage. Also referred to as an All-Inclusive Trust Deed or AITD.

Yield Ratio, expressed as a percentage, of income from an investment to the total cost of the investment over a given period of time.

Zoning Act of city or county authorities specifying how property may be used in specific areas.

INDEX